Endorsed by

WJEC GCSE English Language

For Wales

Natalie Simpson

Julie Swain

Consultant:
Barry Childs

OXFORD
UNIVERSITY PRESS

OXFORD
UNIVERSITY PRESS

Great Clarendon Street, Oxford, OX2 6DP, United Kingdom

Oxford University Press is a department of the University of Oxford. It furthers the University's objective of excellence in research, scholarship, and education by publishing worldwide. Oxford is a registered trade mark of Oxford University Press in the UK and in certain other countries

First published in 2016

British Library Cataloguing in Publication Data

Data available

ISBN 978-019-836713-0

10 9 8 7 6 5 4 3

Printed in China by Golden Cup

Acknowledgements

The authors and publisher are grateful for permission to reprint extracts from the following copyright material:

Douglas Adams: *The Restaurant and the End of the Universe* (Pan, 2009), copyright © Douglas Adams 1980, reprinted by permission of Pan Macmillan UK, Macmillan Publishers Ltd and Ed Victor Ltd for the Estate of Douglas Adams.

Margaret Atwood: *Oryx and Crake* (Bloomsbury, 2003), copyright © O W Toad Ltd 2003, reprinted by permission of Bloomsbury Publishing Plc,

Gupareet Bains: 'Toad in the Hole' from *The Superfood Diet* (Absolute Press, 2014), copyright © Gupareet Bains 2014, reprinted by permission of Bloomsbury Publishing Plc.

Suzanne Collins: *The Hunger Games: Catching Fire* (Scholastic Press, 2009), copyright © Suzanne Collins, 2009, reprinted by permission of Scholastic, Inc.

Beverley Downes: restaurant review - Ffresh, July 2012 on www.eatsforwales.co.uk, reprinted by permission of the author.

Andrew Lane: *Death Cloud, Young Sherlock Holmes* (Macmillan Children's Books, 2010), copyright © Andrew Lane 2010, reprinted by permission of Macmillan Publishers Ltd.

Stuart Maconie: *Pies and Prejudice: in search of the North* (Ebury Press, 2008), reprinted by permission of The Random House Group Ltd.

Sara Maitland: *A Book of Silence* (Granta, 2008), copyright © Sara Maitland 2008, reprinted by permission of Granta Books.

Ronnie O'Sullivan: *Running* (Orion, 2014), copyright © Ronnie O'Sullivan 2014, reprinted by permission of the Orion Publishing Group

Kira Salak: *The Cruelest Journey* (National Geographic Books, 2004), copyright © Kira Salak 2005, reprinted by arrangement with the National Geographic Society.

Alan Sillitoe: *The Loneliness of the Long-distance Runner* (HarperPerennial, 2007), copyright © Alan Sillitoe1959, reprinted by permission of HarperCollins Publishers Ltd.

Ahdaf Soueif: *The Map of Love* (Bloomsbury, 1999), copyright © Ahdaf Soueif 1999, reprinted by permission of Bloomsbury Publishing plc.

and to the following for their permission to reprint from copyright material:

Table from Children's Dental Health Survey 2013 is Crown © copyright 2013 and is used under the terms of the Open Government Licence v3.0.

Jens Jakob Andersen for infographic 'Growth in Popularity of marathon running' from www.runrepeat.com.

Bloomsbury Publishing plc for back cover description of *The World's Toughest Endurance Challenges* by Richard Hoad and Paul Moore (Bloomsbury Sport, 2012).

British Dental Health Foundation for 'Get Ready to Smile: Fun Facts about Oral Health' poster from www.nationalsmilemonth.org.

Daily Post Wales, Trinity Mirror Group for 'More than 400 food outlets rated "sub-standard" across North Wales', Wales Online at www.wales online.co.uk.

Dorling Kindersley Ltd for 'A Rainbow of Phytonutrients' from *The Neal's Yard Remedies Healing Foods* (DK Adult Life, 2013), copyright © Dorling Kindersley 2013.

Extreme Element Ltd for interview with Nina Nordling of *High Heaven* by Aaron Thomas, 20 Jan 2014.

Guardian News and Media for Snowdonia's dark side - the mega zip wire beneath North Wales' by Rachel Dixon, *The Guardian*, 15 March 2015, copyright © Guardian News & Media 2015; 'Experience: my microwave nearly killed me' by Julia Gatica, *The Guardian*, 8 Aug 2014, copyright © Guardian News & Media 2014; 'Meet the ice mile: the toughest swimming test on the planet' by Sally Goble, *The Guardian*, 7 Jan 2014, copyright © Guardian News & Media 2014; 'Experience: I was swept away by a flood' by Vanessa Glover, *The Guardian*, 15 June 2013, copyright © Guardian News & Media 2013; 'Philippines: thousands evacuated as Typhoon Haiyan strikes' by Kate Hodal, *The Guardian*, 8 Nov 2013, copyright © Guardian News & Media 2013; 'Sir Ranulph Fiennes to attempt record winter Antarctica trek' by Maev Kennedy, *The Guardian*, 17 Sept 2012, copyright © Guardian News & Media 2012; restaurant review: Ffresh by John Lanchester, *The Guardian*, 24 Feb 2012, copyright © Guardian News & Media 2012; 'Laura Trott sick to the stomach in pursuit of 2012 glory' by Donald McRae, *The Guardian*, 6 Feb 2012, copyright © Guardian News & Media 2012; 'Free runners hit the streets as urban craze sweeps Britain' by Ben Quinn & David Smith, *The Guardian*, 3 Aug 2008, copyright © Guardian News & Media 2008; and 'A Parkrun is an unusual, even beautiful sight' by Ben Smith, *The Guardian*, 11 March 2013, copyright © Guardian News & Media 2013.

James Grant Media Management for transcript of speech by Declan Donnelly and Anthony McPartlin (Ant and Dec) on ITV National Television Awards 2013, after being awarded the *Landmark Achievement Award* for 25 years in show business.

NHS Choices for 'Get running with Couch to 5K' from the HNS Choices website at www.nhs.uk.

News Syndication for 'Base Jumpers: the men who fall to earth' by Ed Caesar, *Sunday Times*, 8 March 2009, copyright © Ed Caesar/ News UK and Ireland Ltd 2009; and 'Extreme weather in 2012 could be a record' by Oliver Moody, *The Times*, 3 March 2013, copyright © Oliver Moody/ News UK and Ireland Ltd 2013.

Nations Restaurant News Penton Media via Copyright Clearance Center for table: 'Top superfoods offered at restaurants' from *Nations Restaurant News*, April 2013, www.nrn.com.

The Random House Group Ltd for back cover description of *Great Outdoor Adventure* by Bear Grylls (Channel 4 Books, 2008).

Rother and Wealdon Councils for 'What to look for when eating out' from www.rother.gov.uk.

Solo Syndication/ Mail Online for 'Other nurses clock on and off - she is constant' by Linda Sturgis, Mail Online, 28 March 2013, copyright © 2013; 'and 'Swashbucking Sherlock' film review by Chris Tookey of *Sherlock Holmes: A Game of Shadows, Mail Online*, 16 Dec 2011, copyright © 2011.

Telegraph Media Group for 'Rotten teeth are all the fault of Mum and Dad' by Victoria Lambert, *The Telegraph*, 15 July 2014, copyright © Telegraph Media Group Ltd 2014; and 'The fearful adventurer: confronting my demons at the world's highest bungee jump' by Tobias Mews, *Daily Telegraph*, 19 Dec 2013, copyright © Telegraph Media Group Ltd 2013.

Although we have made every effort to trace and contact all copyright holders before publication this has not been possible in all cases. If notified, the publisher will rectify any errors or omissions at the earliest opportunity.

The authors and publisher would like to thank the following for permissions to use their photographs:

Cover: Wong Hock weng/Shutterstock; **p8:** © RooM the Agency/Alamy; **p10:** EpicStockMedia/ Shutterstock; © Aurora Photos/Alamy; © Eureka/Alamy; **p11:** IM_photo/Shutterstock; **p12:** Christophe Michot/Shutterstock; **p13:** Shahid Ali Khan/Shutterstock; **p14-15:** © Bryan Sinclaire/Alamy; **p15:** © ClassicStock/Alamy; **p16:** © Maskot/Alamy; **p17:** With kind permission of GoBelow; **p18:** salajean/Shutterstock; **p20:** charles taylor/Shutterstock; **p21:** Courtesy of Aerial Extreme, www.aerialextreme.co.uk; Michal Vitek/Shutterstock; **p22:** Radin Myroslav/Shutterstock; Courtesy of Jungle Marathon, www.junglemarathon.com; **p23:** © Travelscape Images/Alamy; **p24:** Danuta Hyniewska/Getty Images; **p25:** mexrix/Shutterstock; **p26:** Alexei Zinin/Shutterstock; **p27:** Darrenp/Shutterstock; Vitalii Nesterchuk/Shutterstock; **p28:** Will Ireland/Future Publishing via Getty Images; **p29:** © Life's Like That/Alamy; **p31:** Nigel Kirby/LOOP IMAGES/Loop Images/Corbis; **p33:** JHDT Stock Images LLC/Shutterstock; **p35:** © Glenn Millington/Alamy; **p36:** Richard Whitcombe/Shutterstock; **p37:** Richard Whitcombe/Shutterstock; **p38-39:** andrej pol/Shutterstock; **p40:** © MBI/Alamy; **p43:** Stepan Popov/iStock; **p45:** Aleksey Stemmer/Shutterstock; Chris Winter/LNP/REX Shutterstock; **p46:** Courtesy of Friends of the Earth; **p46:** Reproduction of the "WE ARE MACMILLAN CANCER SUPPORT" logo and strapline is by kind permission of UK charity Macmillan Cancer Support.; **p47:** © Paul Kingsley/Alamy; **p48:** Maggy Meyer/Shutterstock; Anton Ivanov/Shutterstock; Galyna Andrushko/Shutterstock; **p49:** © Jim Holden/Alamy; **p50:** Paket/Shutterstock; **p51:** Artwork © Discovery Channel. Used by arrangement with The Random House Group Limited.; **p53:** Byelikova Oksana/Shutterstock; **p55:** Karol Kozlowski/iStockphoto; **p57:** Courtesy of Aerial Extreme, www.aerialextreme.co.uk; **p60:** Greg Epperson/Shutterstock; **p62-63:** © Jan Wlodarczyk/Alamy; **p64:** Early Spring/Shutterstock; Napat/Shutterstock; **p65:** joannawnuk/ Shutterstock; **p66:** Penguin Random House UK; **p66;** (from top) Maks Narodenko/Shutterstock; Valentyn Volkov/Shutterstock; Tim UR/Shutterstock; da_yama/Shutterstock; Binh Thanh Bui/ Shutterstock; **p67:** yingtustocker/Shutterstock; **p67:** MRS.Siwaporn/Shutterstock; **p69:** © Sebastian Kaulitzki/Alamy; **p71:** MyFitnessPal.com; **p72:** MyFitnessPal.com; **p73:** Q2A Media; **p73:** Q2A Media; **p72:** Wilunda Mayurakul/Shutterstock; **p74:** Martin Valigursky/Shutterstock; **p75:** bonchan/Shutterstock; **p77:** Foodio/Shutterstock; **p78:** Jozef Sowa/Shutterstock; **p79:** lzf/ Shutterstock; Sergey Novikov/Shutterstock; **p80:** c.W.Disney/Everett/REX Shutterstock; **p83:** © Design Pics Inc/Alamy; **p84:** © Photos 12/Alamy; **p85:** © foodfolio/Alamy; **p87:** © isobel flynn/Alamy; **p88-89:** Maria Starovoytova/Shutterstock; **p90:** Syda Productions/Shutterstock; **p92:** FSA - www.food.gov.uk; **p93:** © Eugenio Franchi/Alamy; **p95:** © Isabella Cassini/Alamy; © Realimage/Alamy; **p96:** Africa Studio/Shutterstock; **p98:** Syda Productions/Shutterstock; **p100:** Leonardo da/Shutterstock; **p101:** © Lumi Images/Alamy; **p103:** © Jeff Morgan 16/ Alamy; **p105:** © Jon Parker Lee/Alamy; **p106-107:** Rawpixel.com/Shutterstock; **p108:** ANDRZEJ GRZEGORCZYK/Shutterstock; Jon Arnold Images Ltd/Alamy; Rawpixel.com/Shutterstock; **p109:** efecreata mediagroup/Shutterstock; Dfree/Shutterstock; © David Cole/Alamy; Camilo Torres/Shutterstock; **p110:** © World History Archive/Alamy; **p111:** © Photos 12/Alamy; © AF archive/Alamy; © AF archive/Alamy; **p112:** REX/Hartswood Films; **p113:** ostill/Shutterstock; **p114:** Tatyana Borodina/Shutterstock; betto rodrigues/Shutterstock; c.Warner Br/Everett/REX Shutterstock; **p115:** Marine's/Shutterstock; **p116:** © AF archive/Alamy; **p117:** Shane White/ Shutterstock; **p119:** Migel/Shutterstock; **p120:** Moviestore Collection/REX Shutterstock; **p123:** Courtesy of http://www.firefightersneeded.tv/; © RubberBall/Alamy; **p124:** © Chris Pancewicz/ Alamy; **p128:** David Fisher/REX Shutterstock; **p130:** © PAUL HANNA/Reuters/Corbis; **p132:** Alina555/iStock; **p133:** London News Pictures/REX Shutterstock; **p134:** Ken McKay/REX Shutterstock; © Jamie Beeden/Corbis; Brian J. Ritchie/Hotsauce/REX Shutterstock; **p136-137:** © Design Pics Inc/Alamy; **p138:** © Eric Farrelly/Alamy; © D Hale-Sutton/Alamy; © Colin Underhill/ Alamy; **p142-143:** everything possible/Shutterstock; **p145:** Jaroslaw Grudzinski/Shutterstock; © epa european pressphoto agency b.v./Alamy; **p146:** Noel Moore/Shutterstock; c.20thC.Fox/ Everett/REX Shutterstock; **p147:** michaket/Shutterstock; © Art Directors & TRIP/Alamy; **p149:** Jaroslav74/Shutterstock; **p151:** Alexander Raths/Shutterstock; **p152:** © dpa picture alliance/ Alamy; **p153:** Pixsooz/Shutterstock; **p163:** CBsigns /Alamy Stock Photo; Crdjan/Shutterstock; **p172:** Sharlotta/Shutterstock.

Page layout by Kamae Design.

This material has been endorsed by WJEC and offers high quality support for the delivery of WJEC qualifications. While this material has been through a WJEC quality assurance process, all responsibility for the content remains with the publisher.

CONTENTS

WJEC GCSE English Language specification overview

The exam papers

The grade you receive at the end of your WJEC GCSE English Language course is based on your performance in two exam papers and your non-examination assessment, Oracy. The following provides a summary of the two exam papers:

Exam paper	Reading and Writing questions and marks	Assessment Objectives	Timing	Marks (and % of GCSE)
Unit 2: Reading and Writing: Description, Narration and Exposition	**Section A: Reading** Understanding at least one description, one narration and one exposition text, including continuous and non-continuous texts Exam questions and marks: • Range of structured questions (40 marks)	Reading: • AO2	2 hours	Reading: 40 marks (20% of GCSE) Writing: 40 marks (20% of GCSE) Paper 1 total: 80 marks (40% of GCSE)
	Section B: Writing Extended writing, drawing upon texts from Section A as appropriate Exam questions and marks: • Proofreading task focusing on writing accurately (5 marks) • One writing task selected from a choice of two that could be description, narration or exposition (20 marks are awarded for communication and organization; 15 marks are awarded for writing accurately)	Writing: • AO3		
Unit 3: Reading and Writing: Argumentation, Persuasion and Instructional	**Section A: Reading** Understanding of at least one argumentation, one persuasion and one instructional text, including continuous and non-continuous texts Exam questions and marks: • Range of structured short response and extended response questions (35 marks)	Reading: • AO2	2 hours	Reading: 40 marks (20% GCSE) Writing: 40 marks (20% GCSE) Paper 2 total: 80 marks (40% of GCSE)
	Section B: Writing Extended writing, drawing upon texts from Section A as appropriate Exam questions and marks: • One compulsory argumentation writing task (10 marks are awarded for communication and organization; 10 marks are awarded for writing accurately) • One compulsory persuasion writing task (10 marks are awarded for communication and organization; 10 marks are awarded for writing accurately)	Writing: • AO3		

Spoken Language

As well as preparing for the two GCSE English Language exams,
your course also includes a spoken language assessment, Oracy.

Exam paper	Spoken Language questions and marks	Assessment Objectives	Marks (and % of GCSE)
Unit 1: Non-examination assessment Oracy	**Task 1: Individual Researched Presentation** One individual presentation based on an aspect of a set theme	Oracy ● AO1	40 marks (10% GCSE))
	Task 2: Responding and Interacting Group discussion based on written and/or visual stimuli provided by WJEC		40 marks (10% GCSE)

The Assessment Objectives

AO1	● Present and organize information clearly and purposefully, sustaining and adapting their talk in formal and informal situations using a variety of techniques and verbal reasoning skills as appropriate. ● Listen and respond appropriately to other speakers' ideas, questions and perspectives, and how they construct and express meanings. ● Interact with others, shaping meaning through suggestions, comments and questions and drawing ideas together. ● Use a range of appropriate sentence structures appropriately for clarity, purpose and effect, with accurate grammar and expression. *Half of the available credit for AO1 will be awarded for the choice of appropriate register, grammatical accuracy and range of sentence structures with the remainder for content and organization.*
AO2	● Use inference and deduction skills to retrieve and analyse information from a wide range of written texts. ● Synthesize and summarize information from a range of texts. ● Interpret themes, meaning, ideas and information in a range of texts and challenging writing. ● Edit texts and compare and evaluate the usefulness, relevance and presentation of content within or across texts. ● Refer to evidence within texts, distinguishing between statements that are supported by evidence and those that are not. ● Evaluate and reflect on the ways in which texts may be interpreted differently according to the perspective of the reader and distinguishing between facts or evidence and opinions, bias and argument. ● Understand and recognize the purpose and reliability of texts, e.g. texts for personal, public, occupational and educational use.
AO3	▪ Write to communicate clearly and effectively, using and adapting register and forms and selecting vocabulary and style appropriate to task and purpose in ways that engage the reader. ▪ Proofread, and use linguistic, grammatical, structural and presentational features in their own writing to achieve particular effects, to engage and influence the reader and to support overall coherence. ▪ Use a range of sentence structures and paragraphs appropriately for clarity, purpose and effect, with accurate grammar, punctuation and spelling. *Half of the marks for this section will be awarded for communication and organization (meaning, purpose, readers and structure) and the other for writing accurately.*

> **A note on spelling**
> Certain words, for example 'synthesize' and 'organize', have been spelt
> with 'ize' throughout this book. It is equally acceptable to spell these
> words with 'ise'.

How this book will help you

Develop your reading and writing skills

The primary aim of this book is to develop and improve your reading and writing skills. Crucially however, in this book you will be doing this in the context of what the exam papers will be asking of you at the end of your course. So, the skills you will be practising throughout this book are ideal preparation for your two English Language exam papers.

Explore the types of texts that you will face in the exams

In your English Language exams you will have to respond to a number of unseen texts. In order to prepare you fully for the range and types of text that you might face in the exam, this book is structured thematically so you can explore the connections between texts. This is ideal preparation for your exams as the unseen texts in your exam papers will be of different types (fiction and non-fiction) and will in some instances be connected.

Become familiar with the Assessment Objectives and the exam paper requirements

Assessment Objectives are the skills that underpin all qualifications. Your GCSE English Language exam papers are testing six Assessment Objectives (see page 5). Chapters 1 to 3 of this book take exactly the same approach – each chapter develops your reading and writing skills addressing the same Assessment Objectives. Chapter 4 pulls all the skills together that you have been practising in order to help prepare you for 'mock' exam papers at the end of the book.

Practise the types of task you will face in the exams

Chapters 1 to 3 in this book include substantial end-of-chapter assessments that enable you to demonstrate what you have learnt and help your teacher assess your progress. Each of these assessments includes tasks that prepare you for the types of task that you will be facing in your GCSE English Language exams. The sample papers at the end of the book give you the opportunity to bring together all that you have been learning and practising in a 'mock' exam situation.

How is the book structured?

Chapters 1 to 3

Chapters 1 to 3 develop your reading and writing skills within different themes. Each chapter opens with an introductory page that introduces the theme, explains the skills you will be developing and links the learning to the exam requirements.

Across the chapters you will be developing responses in the context of all of the reading Assessment Objectives and across the chapters you will encounter all of the text types that your exam paper texts will be taken from.

Your writing skills are also developed throughout every chapter, including a focus on improving your technical accuracy (also known as SPAG – Spelling, Punctuation and Grammar).

Chapter 4

Chapter 4 pulls all of the skills together that you have learnt throughout the course, revisiting key points and providing you with revision practise. The chapter and book concludes with sample exam papers to enable you and your teacher to see how much progress you have made.

What are the main features within this book?

Activities, Stretch and Support

To develop your reading responses to the wide range of texts included in this book as well as developing your writing skills, you will find many varied activities. The 'Support' feature provides additional help with the activity whilst the 'Stretch' feature introduces further challenge to help develop a more advanced response.

Tips, Key terms and glossed words

These features help support your understanding of key terms, concepts and more difficult words within a source text. These therefore enable you to concentrate fully on developing your reading and writing skills.

Exam link and Progress check

The exam link box explains how the skills you are developing relate to the exam papers. In addition to the summative end of chapter assessments, you will also find regular formative assessments in the form of 'Progress checks'. Through peer or self assessment, these enable you to assess your learning and establish next steps and targets.

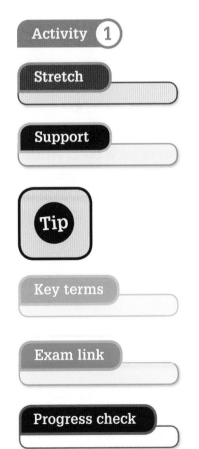

1 EXTREMES

In your English exam you will read a range of texts. These texts have been written in a variety of different styles for different purposes and audiences. This chapter will help to familiarize you with the kinds of texts and purposes which you may face in your exams.

'Tell the truth, or someone will tell it for you.'
Stephanie Klein

'I enjoy doing the research of non-fiction; that gives me some pleasure, being a detective again.'
Joseph Wambaugh

'In non-fiction, you have that limitation, that constraint, of telling the truth.'
Peter Matthiessen

Introduction

The focus of this chapter is 'Extremes'. In the exam, Unit 2 and Unit 3 will be based on a theme and the style of this chapter will help to familiarize you with thematically linked texts.

You will examine how extremes can be presented and will have the opportunity to reflect on what makes an event extreme and how extreme events can make a reader feel and react. While you are working through the chapter, try to consider the impact of these extremes both on the people experiencing them and on the world around them.

Exam link

Exam relevance

Think carefully about word meaning and how words and definitions can help you to understand meaning as you will be asked to suggest what certain words and phrases mean in Units 2 and 3.

Exploring extremes

Learning objectives

- To explore the theme of extremes
- To consider your own experience of extremes

For our purposes, 'extreme' can be defined in two ways.

As an **adjective** it can mean:

- very great or intense
- furthest away, outermost: *the extreme edge*
- going to great lengths in actions or opinions, not moderate.

As a **noun** it can mean:

- either end of something
- something extreme, either of two concepts or opinions that are as different from each other as they can be.

Activity 1

Consider what the word 'extreme' means to you:

- Think about your own experiences of extremes. Write down any words or phrases that you associate with this idea.
- Discuss with a friend the ways you think this word can be used. Share your ideas and write down any new ones.
- Using the ideas you have discussed, write your own definition for 'extreme'.

Activity 2

Look at the images on this page. What can you see? Why do you think these pictures could be described as extreme? Write down any words or phrases you would use to describe the extremes pictured in them.

Activity 3

Choose one of the images from Activity 2. Imagine you are the photographer who took the photograph and answer the following questions.

1. Why did you take the photograph?
2. Where were you when you took the photograph?
3. Describe the weather conditions in your location.
4. Write down five words or phrases to describe how this picture makes you feel.

Key terms

SPAG

Adjectives: words like *big*, *exciting* and *unexpected*. They describe what is named by nouns, noun phrases or pronouns
Nouns: words like *girl*, *book*, *Mary*, *school*, *year*, *money*, *happiness*, *Brighton*. One of their main jobs is to identify a person, place or thing

The language or words you chose may have helped to convey the extreme nature of the location. Choosing language carefully is essential when writing, as it allows your reader to picture what you are describing. If you are describing an extreme environment or location, you should think about choosing words and phrases that express intensity.

Activity 4

Think about the TV programmes you have watched, the news reports you have read or listened to, or any books you have read. All of these will have, at some time, included information about extremes. During the last week you may have come across some extreme events or people. Even the weather can be described as extreme if it is unusually severe. Can you think of any other situations where you may have encountered extremes?

Design and complete a table with four specific examples to show your recent experiences of extremes in non-fiction. For example:

Source of extremes	What happened
BBC News	Deadly heatwaves and devastating floods have sparked popular interest in understanding the role of global warming in driving extreme weather.

Think carefully about the words and phrases you choose to convey the intensity of the situation.

Extreme sports

1 Reading techniques

Learning objectives

- To develop reading skills
- To understand different ways of gathering information when you read

Key terms

Perspective: a particular way of thinking about something

Purpose: the purpose of a text is what the writer deliberately sets out to achieve. They may wish to persuade, encourage, advise or even anger their reader, or a mixture of these

Topic sentence: often the first sentence in a paragraph, it tells the reader what the paragraph is about, and is followed by other sentences which give more detail

Fact: something that is known to have happened and/or to be true

Introduction

In recent years, extreme sports have become increasingly popular. Although many people think they are dangerous, for participants they produce high levels of adrenaline, excitement and challenge. In this unit you will learn new skills and improve on your existing reading skills, using texts about extreme sports to inspire you.

Because we learn to read when we are young, reading becomes a skill that we rarely think about. Being able to read and understand a text is a crucial skill for life, school and exams. When reading a text, there are a number of different techniques that you can use:

Close reading
This will enable you to understand a text in detail. It will help you to understand the writer's overall meaning and **perspective**, and the **purpose** of the text. When you read closely you need to try to understand each sentence and what the writer is trying to convey.

Skimming
This is much quicker than close reading. When you skim a text, you do not read every word but try to take in the overall meaning and organizational structure of the text by moving your eyes throughout the passage. Headings and **topic sentences** are really useful for this technique – these features help you to locate main ideas, topics or information quickly.

Scanning
You use this technique if you are looking for a particular piece of information or a key word. If you were asked to find out why an event was dangerous, you could begin by scanning the text for the word *danger*. This technique is useful if you are asked to locate a **fact** or phrase.

Activity 1

Read the extract 'Base jumpers: the men who fall to earth'. It includes some difficult words and phrases that you may not understand. Your teacher may ask you to write these down and try to work out what they mean. Even though a text may have some complicated sections, if you read closely you can usually work out the *overall* meaning and the meaning of key words and phrases. In the exam you may face multiple choice questions to test your understanding of meaning. Close reading practice can help you improve this skill.

Base jumpers: the men who fall to earth

What would drive someone to risk life, limb and liberty by breaking into the world's tallest building and jumping off the top of it with just one small parachute? Ed Caesar infiltrates[1] the secret society of the death-defying base jumpers.

In the early hours of April 9, 2008, a 44-year-old Englishman and a 48-year-old Frenchman sat silently on the edge of the windowless 155th floor of the Burj tower – the tallest building in the world – watching dawn bleed over Dubai. From their eyrie[2] half a mile up, they saw the desert turn from blue to pink and heard the muezzins[3] call the faithful to prayer. In that moment, remembers the Frenchman, 'everything below seemed to belong to us. We felt like kings, and this was our kingdom'.

Their reign was short. At 5.30am, the men could see truckloads of workers arriving at the site, ready to start construction for the day. It was time to go. They rose to their feet. The Englishman looked at his friend, counted to three, and launched himself from the building. The Frenchman followed a moment later.

The Englishman fell like a shot pheasant for ten long seconds. He then drew his small pilot chute, which caught, filled with air, and released the blossom of his main canopy. The Frenchman took more time. He was wearing a wingsuit – a webbed overall that allows a parachutist to travel forward as well as down. As he fell, he spread his arms wide, raised his chest to the dawn, and glided away from the building. When he had flown as close as he dared to a nearby skyscraper, he deployed[4] his parachute and descended[5] to safety. The pair had done it – they had pulled off one of the greatest coups[6] in the history of base jumping. Why? Why would someone be so stupid as to jump from a building with only a small parachute on their back? An answer (perhaps not the answer, but an answer) is that people have been doing this kind of thing, if not for ever, then at least for 150 years. Ever since Charles Blondin strutted across Niagara Falls on a tightrope in 1859, ever since Houdini first broke from his shackles, ever since the most famous wirewalker of all, the Man on Wire, Philippe Petit, danced between the twin towers in 1974, men – and it is almost always men – have needed to touch the void.

[1]infiltrate – to enter a place or organization gradually and without being noticed
[2]eyrie – the nest of an eagle or other bird of prey
[3]muezzin – a Muslim crier who proclaims the hours of prayer from a minaret

[4]deploy – to bring something into effective action
[5]descend – to move down
[6]coup – a sudden and unexpected successful action

Activity ②

Once you have read the extract, think about what you have learned about base jumping and what the writer thinks about it. Now discuss the following with a partner.

- What do you learn about base jumping from this article?
- Why do you think Ed Caesar wrote this text?
- If you had to tell someone about this text in 50 words, what would you say?

Exam link

Being able to summarize information from a text is an important exam skill. Start by reading the text closely and picking out only the key details.

Activity

Now you need to use skimming and scanning reading skills to retrieve the following information from the extract on page 13. Some tips have been provided to help focus your search. See how quickly you can find the information.

1. What is base jumping?
2. When did the event take place?
3. How did the Frenchman feel?
4. What was the Frenchman wearing?
5. Write down any words that show how Ed Caesar feels about the jump.

Tip

1. A definition of base jumping is crucial to understanding the extract, so start at the beginning and skim the text. Don't forget to look at the title.
2. Looking at the **topic sentence** for each paragraph is a good place to start.
3. Scan the text and look for the word *feel* or *felt*.
4. Scan the text looking for the word *wearing*.
5. Skim back through the whole passage looking for any words that might suggest his opinion about the jump.

The language or words and phrases used by a writer help a reader to understand exactly what is being said. Writers are often deliberate in the language they choose. Carefully selected language can paint a clear image for a reader so they can visualize what the writer is describing. Language can also make a reader feel a range of emotions such as anger, sympathy and surprise.

Activity 4

Look at the following phrases about base jumpers and see if you can work out why the writer has chosen specific words.

> 'watching dawn bleed over Dubai'

What does the word 'bleed' suggest about the colour of the morning sun? What does it suggest about how the colour is merging with the rest of the sky?

> 'fell like a shot pheasant'

What is your image of the pheasant? How do you think it is falling, given the fact that it has been shot?

> 'the blossom of his main canopy'

Why has the writer used the word 'blossom' to describe the parachute? What image do you get of the shape of the parachute?

Tip When exploring word meaning read the whole sentence in which the word appears as this may give you some additional details to help you to deduce its meaning. If given a multiple choice question, work through the options carefully, discarding any which do not work.

2 **Exploring texts**

Learning objectives

- To locate and **retrieve** information from texts
- To explore word meaning
- To understand what is meant by synthesis

Key terms

Retrieve: to find or extract; to locate and bring back

Summary: a brief document or statement that gives the main points of something. It is a shortened version of a longer text which is written up in the reader's own words. Producing a summary tests your understanding of what you have read

Being able to extract key information from a text is crucial not only in English but in wider life. Extracting key points will help you to:

- understand the meaning of a text
- answer retrieval questions in your exam
- produce a **summary** or overview of a text.

Activity 1

Read Extract 1, 'Leap of Faith?' below and use your retrieval skills to answer the following questions. Remember to include only relevant information to answer each question:

1. Where can you find Zip Below Xtreme?
2. Before Zip Below Xtreme existed, what could be found at the location?
3. To what depth can members of the public explore?
4. What age do you have to be to enjoy a full-day adventure?

Extract 1

◀ ▶ ⟳ ✕ + _____ · Q⟲

Leap of Faith?

This leap of faith is the climax of Zip Below Xtreme, a new underground adventure near Betws-y-Coed in Snowdonia, north Wales. The setting is an abandoned slate mine, and the route lends itself to superlatives: the longest underground adventure (5km); the longest underground zipline (130 metres); the deepest publicly accessible point in the UK (almost 400 metres). The trip entails a whole day below ground, and is for over-18s only (though there is an easier half-day version for over-10s).

Activity ②

1. What does 'superlative' mean?

2. The writer uses the word 'superlatives' in the text. When you are reading you have to work like a detective to find out what words mean. Follow the tips below.

   - The writer uses the plural 'superlative**s**' so you are looking for more than one thing.
   - A colon follows the word 'superlatives' so a list will follow.

   a) What do you notice about the list? Are there any common or similar words (longest, deepest)?

   b) What do you think a superlative could be?

3. Remind yourself of the definition of a summary.

   In no more than 15 words, try to summarize what Zip Below Xtreme is.

The extract on the next page is taken from the same article. Read the extract then complete Activity 3 that follows.

Exam link

In the exam you will be given approximately five to six linked texts. The texts may offer a range of opinions on a given topic and will be written for a range of different purposes. The texts will be continuous or non-continuous.

- Continuous texts involve prose organized in sentences and paragraphs – one sentence or more is seen as a continuous text.
- Non-continuous texts present information in other ways, such as in lists, forms, graphs or diagrams.

Tip When producing your summary, think about the location (an abandoned mine). Think about what you do there (adventure). List a series of key words from the text but do not copy whole phrases or sentences.

Extract 2

'The free fall is very scary. I did it five times in a row to try to get used to it, but it was still just as frightening the fifth time as the first.' The words of Pete, a caving instructor and former soldier who fought in Afghanistan, are ringing in my ears as I stand at the top of a 21-metre abyss. The thin beam of light from my head torch barely penetrates the darkness; it is just enough to make out the edge of the cliff and the black nothingness below. I count to three – and step off.

Activity 3

Below are two exam-style questions that test your understanding of word meaning. Having read Extract 2 carefully, answer both of them.

1. In your own words, explain what the word 'penetrate' means.

2. Explain what is meant by the word 'abyss'. Choose one of the following four options:

   a) A very dark and frightening place ☐

   b) A long ladder ☐

   c) A zip wire platform ☐

   d) A deep or bottomless void ☐

Tip When answering multiple choice questions first read the sentence in which the word is contained and see if you can work out what it means. Next read the multiple choice options and eliminate the distractors before selecting the correct answer.

Stretch

Read Extract 2 again. Explain why the writer tells us that Pete 'fought in Afghanistan'? List as many possible reasons as you can think of.

In the examination you may be asked to **synthesize** information from two sources. When producing a synthesis you need to read the task carefully to help you understand exactly which pieces of information you will need to extract from the source materials.

Key term

Synthesize: to form something by bringing together information from different sources

Activity 4

Re-read Extracts 1 and 2 on pages 16 and 18. Synthesizing information from the two texts, write down what people will encounter when they visit this attraction.

Tip When producing a synthesis try to put the information into your own words but remember to use the facts from the text.

(3) Recognizing different text types

Learning objectives

- To revise different text types
- To understand what different texts look like and the types of features they might include
- To analyse the presentation of different texts

Key terms

Formal: strictly following accepted social rules; traditional, proper. A piece of formal writing is addressed to someone you are either unfamiliar with or to a formal audience, for example, a school teacher or governor

Informal: not formal; unofficial or casual; everyday. A piece of informal writing is addressed to someone you are familiar or friends with

In the exam you will be asked to read and produce a range of text types. Some of the texts you will face will be classed as: description, narration, exposition, argumentation, persuasion and instructional. Writers often have to produce a particular type of text. For example, a journalist will produce articles for a newspaper or magazine, while a school may use a letter or email format to send information home.

Activity 1

Look at the extracts on pages 21–23. These are some of the kinds of popular texts you encounter in everyday life. Look at the features of each extract carefully. Can you match the definitions below to the extracts on pages 21–23?

A Article – a short, self-contained piece of writing often found in a newspaper or magazine.

B Blog – a website where someone writes about their own opinions, activities and experiences. Blogs are usually structured so that other people can comment or begin discussions about the topics included in the blog.

C Webpage – a page within a given website that can be found on the Internet.

D Letter – a written message to a specific audience. Letters can be **formal** or **informal**, depending on the audience. The level of formality will determine the style and content of the letter.

E Book extract – a passage or section from a book. An extract may cover an entire event, or it may simply give a character outline or a snapshot of a larger main event.

F Leaflet – a printed sheet of paper giving information, especially one given out for free. Most leaflets are produced to encourage or persuade a reader to do something (for example, to visit an attraction or donate money), or to give out information (for example, a leaflet found at a doctors' surgery about a medical condition like meningitis).

Extract 1

Dear Editor,

I was appalled to read that last weekend's weather not only played havoc with my hydrangeas but that it also sparked what can only be described as a sport for lunatics. For those of you not yet acquainted with this latest craze, let me explain. Tombstoning is the 'art' of diving off rocks, cliffs and bridges into the, often shallow and rocky but almost always dangerous, waters below. This fad has claimed more than twenty lives in the last five years but is growing in popularity…

Extract 2

Extract 3

JAN 20

Expert Interview with Nina Nordling of High Heaven

Extreme News and Views

Hi Nina, thanks for talking to us. We hear you're embarking on a pretty exciting venture this year and we can't wait to hear more about it. Please start by telling us a little about yourself, and how you got into the extreme sports industry:

I started riding motocross a couple of years back, and I discovered I just loved everything to do with adrenaline [...] I founded a motocross team for women and got really interested in the action sports industry, being active in skate, surf and a ton of motorsports, as well as the TV host of the Swedish MX Championships. As a first-time entrepreneur I realized I needed a kickass team and today we are three super-ambitious team members working with the startup High Heaven.

Extract 4

Free runners hit the streets as urban craze sweeps Britain

It's seen on TV and the web, and free running is now soaring in popularity in UK cities. But as schools embrace it and the world championships come to London, critics say it's highly dangerous.

It is one of the hottest days of the summer and outside London's South Bank Centre Jake Penny, 15, and his friend, Joe Scandrett, 13, are hurling themselves around a warren of concrete pedestrian underpasses.

Using ledges, metal handrails and anything else within reach, the two teenagers cause passers-by to gape by executing back-flips and somersaults high into the air, each time landing gracefully and silently on the pavement.

Extract 5

About JM   Runner Forum   Gallery   JM Shop   Links   Contact

★ Brazil Race   Volunteers   Sponsors   Media   Eco   Race '12

"FLONA" Tapajos | Application Form | Itinerary & stages | Prizes | Race Overview | Rules and Regulations | Training | What is Included

JungleMarathon

Welcome to the UVU Jungle Marathon 2013

Voted by CNN as "the World's Toughest Endurance Race"

Can you cope with temperatures of 40c?
Humidity of 99%?
Primary Jungle with a dense canopy covering and not a chink of daylight?
Swamp crossings where anacondas lurk?
River crossings with caiman and piranhas as companions?
Insane elevation, often on slippery muddy slopes?
Sleeping in deep jungle to the sounds of jaguar and howler monkeys?

Only the brave will register.

Whether you do 42km, 122km or 254km, you will NEVER forget this adventure.
If you are not up for it, leave now.

UVU JM 2013 Brazil
Registration Open

🦶 **Enter Online**

Find us on
f Facebook

twitter

Ⓟ

Event Sponsors

Extract 6

Across the world seemingly ordinary people are undertaking extraordinary challenges that will push their limits to achieve the improbable – by sea, bike, foot or sled. From the Badwater Ultramarathon in the unforgiving heat of Death Valley in California to the freezing wilderness of Alaska, these once-in-a-lifetime experiences are increasingly popular, and strangely addictive. For a certain breed of competitor, there is an unbreakable drive to see exactly how much the body and will can endure.

Activity 2

1. Can you think of any other text types? Discuss with a partner and write them down.

2. Write down any features you can think of that these text types might have in common.

3. Look closely at the letter. It is a formal letter; can you see anything that is missing?

Stretch

Select one of the text types and read it closely. Who is the intended audience? What features has the writer used to make it more appealing to the target audience?

4 Interpreting meaning

Learning objectives

- To reflect on what a writer is trying to make you feel
- To explore and evaluate a writer's techniques

Understanding why a person has written a text and what they think about the topic can often help you to explore the text fully.

Activity 1

Read the extract below closely and think about the writer and what they might have thought about when writing this article. Some of this text has been annotated with the techniques the writer has used to get their message across.

SPAG

Imperative verbs command the reader to become engaged with the text.

This is a superlative adjective, used here to suggest that compared to any other race this is the most difficult.

Questions are asked for dramatic effect; 'pain' and 'danger' show that the writer can't comprehend the big attraction of the ice mile and will explain why in the rest of the article.

Similes give vivid comparisons using things we are familiar with so we can clearly imagine what the writer is trying to explain. They use the words 'as' and 'like' to make the comparison.

Lists can be used to show there are multiple reasons.

Meet the ice mile: the toughest swimming test on the planet

There's a new favourite pastime for swimming masochists: doing a mile without stopping in water colder than 5°C. With pain a certainty and the danger very real, what's the big attraction?

A few years ago I travelled to Finland to compete in the Winter Swimming Championships. It was one of their mildest winters for years but, even so, the water was still –0.7°C. Adrenaline got me through the very short race – but afterwards I felt like my hands had been slammed in a car door and that my feet had been pounded by mallets. It was brutal.

For the past 10 years I've been swimming outdoors throughout the winter. I've swum regularly, sometimes gloriously and sometimes painfully, in water gradually dropping to around 1°C or 2°C. [...] People ask me why I do it. I think it's a kind of invigorating, tingling, mad high – and a serious adrenaline rush. I love it. [...]

However there is one thing I have not contemplated, and have absolutely no wish to take part in. It's something that is gaining popularity among outdoor swimmers and endurance athletes around the world. It's a cold-water challenge called the 'ice mile'.

The basic rules for swimming an ice mile are pretty straightforward. Find a body of water that is below 5°C, and swim one mile under supervision wearing only your swimming costume, a pair of goggles and one silicone swimming hat. [...] It's a serious, serious endeavour that should not be taken lightly.

I have no desire whatsoever to swim an ice mile. Swimming a few hundred metres in water much below 10°C is enough of a challenge to me, and hurts like hell. It does to most regular cold-water swimmers. For every degree below 10°C, your feet and hands hurt more, your muscles contract so much it's hard to make your arms and shoulders stretch out to pull your stroke. Your hands splay as you lose motor function. You can have massive ice-cream headaches. And once you stop generating heat while swimming and are out of the water, the recovery is appalling and you can be cold all day. [...]

An ice mile to me seems punishing in the extreme. [...]

I have to admit to thinking that there is something macho about ice milers. It's a level of punishment and pain that I can't fathom and don't want to experience.

Repetition is used to reinforce or stress a point of view.

Use of the personal pronoun 'I' reinforces the personal nature of the experience.

Sometimes a writer will explicitly state their view about something, for example, 'It was brutal.' Sometimes you need to work like a detective and look for clues or unpick words and phrases to help you understand the implicit point the writer is trying to get across.

Activity 2

Titles are carefully worded so you become instantly attracted to the text and continue to read. Look at the words highlighted below. Why do you think the writer may have selected these specific words?

Meet the ice mile: the toughest swimming test on the planet

In an exam situation there isn't time to analyse every single word. The following questions will help you focus on how to pick out explicit and implicit meaning.

Activity 3

Read the article again, recording words or phrases that give a positive or negative **impression** of cold-water swimming.

Positive language	Negative language
gloriously	painfully

Stretch

Choose one or two examples from each column and explain what the words suggest about cold-water swimming.

Exam link

In an exam, you may be asked to explain the effects of words and phrases and you may choose to pick out some words from the text to help you. You must make sure that any explanation of their effect is clear and concise.

Activity 4

The text has been annotated with some techniques we use when explaining how a writer might achieve an effect. For example, the writer may use the question 'With pain a certainty and the danger very real, what's the big attraction?' to emphasize the fact that she can't understand why anyone would willingly experience pain and danger for fun and that she questions the motives for swimming.

For each of the annotations around the extract:

- copy the relevant word or phrase
- copy the technique and explanation
- discuss why you think the writer has chosen to use this phrase and technique
- write down an explanation to show why you think each phrase is effective.

'I felt like my hands had been slammed in a car door'. Similes give vivid comparisons using familiar things so we can clearly imagine what the writer is trying to explain. They use the words 'as' and 'like' to make the comparison.

The simile is effective because we can imagine the intense pain that would be felt from slamming your hand in a car door and can imagine just how painful the swim must have been.

5 Evaluating what a writer feels

Learning objectives

- To interpret the writer's perspective about a given event
- To explore what the writer feels and how they may make a reader feel

When deducing a writer's perspective, you need to understand exactly what that person thinks and feels about their topic.

Bungee jumping involves jumping from a tall structure while tied to an elastic cord. Buildings, bridges and cranes are commonly used, but extreme jumpers have been known to throw themselves from moving objects, such as hot-air balloons or helicopters. The thrill comes from free-falling and then being thrust back into the air as the cord recoils.

Activity 1

1. Imagine you have decided to take part in a bungee jump for charity. Use a table to record how you felt before, during and after your jump.

2. Discuss with a partner why your feelings might change.

Activity 2

1. Look closely at the first section of the newspaper extract opposite ('The fearful adventurer...'). Write down words or phrases that tell you how the writer is feeling.

2. Next to each word or phrase, write down one word that you think sums up how he feels.

3. What effect do these words and phrases have on you?

   For example:

How the writer feels	One-word summary	Effect on reader
'apprehension is beginning to creep in'	uneasy	His nervousness is escalating so we sympathize with him.

Activity 3

Having completed the bungee jump, the writer explains his fear in the second section of the extract ('Fight the fear'). With a partner, make a list of the reasons he gives to explain why he found bungee jumping so difficult.

Stretch

Look back at the two sections of the text. Make a list of any similarities and any differences that you can see. Do you think the writer has changed his writing style and opinion after the bungee jump has taken place?

The fearful adventurer: confronting my demons at the world's highest bungee jump

> See if you can work out what this means by reading the rest of the sentence.

I'm standing a few feet from the edge of the Bloukrans River Bridge. [...] It's famous for being home to the world's highest commercial bungee bridge jump.

My feet have been tied together, and two men are helping me hop to the edge. For the past hour while waiting my turn I've been trying to remain calm, but apprehension is beginning to creep in. I cautiously look down to where the Bloukrans River, several hundred metres below us, snakes its way to the nearby Indian Ocean. I quickly look up. 'Bloody hell', I think to myself. I decide not to look down again, but rather focus on the panoramic view in front of me.

I'm advised to jump outwards as much as possible, so I'll get a better bounce at the end. Is a better bounce a good thing? I'm not sure.

I take a deep breath and try to block out the voice in my head that's screaming, 'It's not too late to change your mind!' But I'm not going to chicken out – after all, I'm only doing this 216m-high escapade for one reason: to rebel against the fear that's begun to grip me as I get older.

The words 'Three, two, one, go!' ring out. I throw caution to the wind and jump.

Fight the fear

There was, of course, absolutely no reason for me to be afraid. Face Adrenalin have seen an average of 110 jumps every day for the past 16 years – with a 100pc safety record. That's 642,400 people who've managed to conquer their fears and, more to the point, survive to tell the tale. [...]

Nonetheless, it was a big deal for me. [...] I've run hundreds of kilometres across deserts in the searing heat, plunged off ferries at dawn into ice-cold black water, skidded along mountain ridges on a bike, and ploughed through heavy jungle foliage – none of which has fazed me too much. I have no problem with the thought of being uncomfortably cold, hot, wet or sleep deprived.

But ask me to jump off a bridge? In an act where I have no control? Well, that requires tapping into an entirely different set of resources and switch off my natural life-protecting instinct. It's something I find increasingly difficult.

Key terms

Speculate: to form an opinion about something without knowing the facts
Reflect: to think deeply or carefully about something

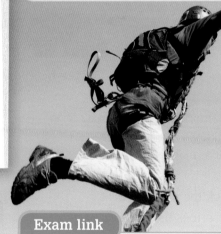

A writer's perspective before an event is often based on their opinions and knowledge about the topic. When a writer has formed an opinion without having experienced something for themselves, they are speculating. We use clues in a text to **speculate** about what might happen.

When a writer has a first-hand experience and then gives their views, this can be classed as factual, since their views are based on something that has happened. The writer in this text **reflects** on what happened and how he feels about it. Good readers can spot the difference between fact and speculation and use this to help them explain the effect of a text.

Exam link

In the exam, the writing task will be linked to the reading texts. Imagine you have been asked to write about a similar experience or activity that made you afraid. Are there any words or phrases you could use from the extract to help you? Does the way the writer structures the text make it seem more dramatic?

6 Purpose

Learning objectives

- To understand what is meant by the purpose of a text
- To work out the purpose of different texts

Exam link

In the exam the questions relating to the purpose of a text will take on a similar format to the one below:

Tick the box that best describes the purpose of this text:

a) Personal use ☐

b) Public use ☐

c) Occupational use ☐

d) Educational use ☐

Texts have many purposes, but in the exam you will be asked to categorize texts as those which are for: personal, public, occupational and educational use. To help you get the question right you must ask yourself what the writer intended the text for.

Activity 1

Read the following definitions and summarize them in your own words:

Personal – written for personal interests but also texts that connect with other people – personal letters, fiction, biography, information texts, personal emails, social media and personal blogs. These texts would often be read during leisure or recreational time as they will be written to satisfy a personal interest.

Public – these texts are produced for people and relate to public activities/issues/concerns. These texts assume anonymous contact with readers. Texts include: official documents, information about public events, discussion-style blogs, news websites and public notices.

Occupational – an occupational reading text is one that is linked to action. It will relate to achieving a goal or task. Occupational texts are described as 'reading to do' and include: job advertisements (where the 'to do' is applying), HR policies and health and safety notices.

Educational – these texts aim to instruct. Educational reading normally requires acquiring information as part of a larger learning task – materials are often not chosen but assigned by an instructor. Printed text books and interactive learning software are typical examples.

Activity 2

The extracts opposite have been taken from texts which have a personal, public, occupational or educational purpose. Read through each example carefully and make a list of any words or phrases that help you to work out the purpose of each text.

Extract 1

… I understand your frustrations with the organization of Dad's 50th birthday party but I'm sure it will be worth it in the end. He's had a tough time this year and I think we need to put our differences behind us. It's not going to be easy but I'm sure we can sort something out.

Extract 2

Superfresh

Fancy a challenge?

Want to do something to raise money for charity?

This year Superfresh employees are invited to compete in the inter-store 'It's a Knockout' challenge. If you'd like to have fun and fancy raising money for a good cause then let us know in no more than 100 words why we should select you to represent us.

Good luck.

Extract 3

We hope you will enjoy your new greenhouse. Prior to construction please ensure you have the following equipment:

Drill   Screwdriver   Hammer   Spanner

Carefully remove sections A and B from the packaging. Place the four longer sections of wood in front of you. There are sixteen smaller sections of wood which are labelled C–R. Place these alongside the corresponding letters along the longer sections of wood…

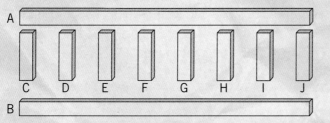

Extract 4

Please note that the station will be closed this weekend due to essential track maintenance and cosmetic repair. We apologize for any convenience caused and hope you will travel with us soon when you will experience added comfort and safety.

Activity 3

Using texts you can find around school, at home or in the classroom, see if you can sort a range of at least six texts according to their purpose.

Stretch

Thinking about the definitions you have read for text purpose, see if you can write **one** text of your own for each text purpose.

Progress check

Think about the stretch activity above. Did you re-read the definitions of each text type before you began? Were you able to work out what to include to produce a brief paragraph for each text type? If you found this difficult, note down which you were unsure about and why.

Go back through the work you completed and underline any words or phrases that link to the text purpose.

Now swap work with a partner. Read through their texts and see if you can work out the purpose for each one.

Extreme weather

7 Exploring text structure

Learning objectives

- To understand text structure
- To consider the different ways that a text can be structured

> **Tip** Always track through a text chronologically (from beginning to end) so you can fully appreciate how the writer's argument develops.

Introduction

Extreme weather is difficult to predict and can cause havoc to both people and environments. In this unit you will develop your writing skills as you analyse and respond to how weather is presented in non-fiction writing. You will also continue to develop some of the reading skills you need for the examination.

Understanding text structure is important. When reading, think about how the writer has put together their ideas. When writing, think carefully about how to bring together information to maximize the effect of your writing on a reader, teacher or examiner. Planning the structure and content of your writing is essential. It will help you to avoid running out of ideas and losing track of your argument.

Features of structure

Within a text, a writer may use one or more of these structural features:

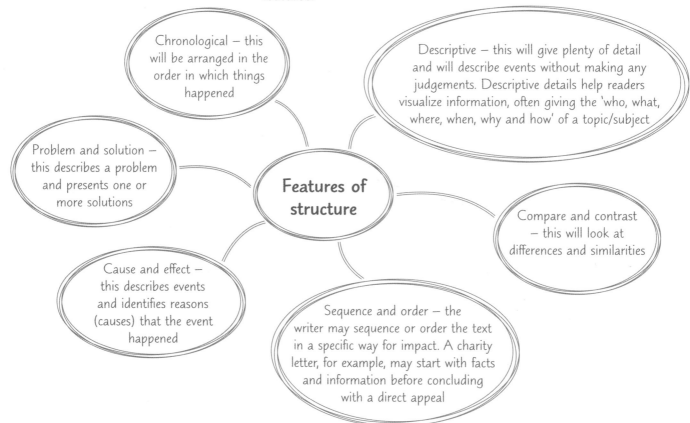

Chronological – this will be arranged in the order in which things happened

Descriptive – this will give plenty of detail and will describe events without making any judgements. Descriptive details help readers visualize information, often giving the 'who, what, where, when, why and how' of a topic/subject

Problem and solution – this describes a problem and presents one or more solutions

Features of structure

Compare and contrast – this will look at differences and similarities

Cause and effect – this describes events and identifies reasons (causes) that the event happened

Sequence and order – the writer may sequence or order the text in a specific way for impact. A charity letter, for example, may start with facts and information before concluding with a direct appeal

Read the following text closely, thinking about the different structural features discussed above as you read.

UK must adapt for weather extremes says Environment Agency

We cannot escape the fact that we have witnessed and experienced some extreme weather in the UK over the past decade. From Hurricane Hercules which attacked much of Cornwall and Wales over the Christmas period in 2013 to the subsequent severe floods which were catastrophic for areas like Sheffield, Salisbury and Dorset, to name but a few. Often the UK seems ill equipped to deal with these weather extremes, but given their frequency and the untold damage they cause, the Environment Agency suggests that urgent action is required.

Almost half the days in 2012 were during either periods of drought or flooding during one of the most extreme years of weather on record, according to Government figures. [...]

The flipside of climate change was also in evidence as dry weather in the later months of 2011 led to widespread drought in the summer of 2012. The Government ordered a hosepipe ban affecting 20 million people and the Environment Agency said 95 days had been in drought, more than a quarter of the year.

More extreme weather is inevitable and will exacerbate many of the problems that we already deal with, including flooding and water scarcity. Taking action today to prepare and adapt homes, businesses, agricultural practices and infrastructure for the future is vital.

Activity 1

1. Look at the four sections which have been highlighted in the extract above. Match the structural features to the correct section of the text.

   A. Compare and contrast   **C.** Cause and effect

   B. Descriptive   **D.** Problem and solution

   Support

   Go back through the text and see if you can find any other structural features from the spider diagram on page 30.

Tip Understanding how a text is structured will help you to answer sequencing tasks.

Stretch

The argument in this text has been carefully structured. Look at each of the examples above and think about what they add to the text and the writer's argument and how they are effective.

Activity 2

1. Look at the exam-style question below and write a list of points that you think would help you to answer the question.

   How does the writer of the article above try to persuade us that the UK needs to adapt for extreme weather?

2. Look at the following section of a sample answer. Consider how you could improve it, then write it out again with your amendments.

   The writer persuades us that we need to adapt to extreme weather because we have seen for ourselves the damage caused, 'we have witnessed and experienced some extreme weather in the UK over the past decade'. The lengthy timescale (ten years) suggests that the problem has been continual and that we need to find a solution.

3. Look back through the passage and your notes. Find three additional examples in the text where the writer persuades us that the UK needs to adapt to extreme weather and add these to the example above.

Tip Work through the extract from the title to the end and think about both the content and structure of the writer's argument. Remember that content includes what the writer has to say and any techniques they use to help them convey their message.

8 The power of words

Learning objectives

- To understand how words and phrases are used in a text
- To consider the effect of specific words and phrases in a text

Writers select words and phrases carefully to influence their readers. When you are looking at a text, identify words and phrases that are significant or relevant, and then think about what the writer is trying to achieve by using them. The language (words) a writer uses can have many different effects. Language that is used to manipulate or evoke the reader's feelings is known as emotive language.

Activity 1

Read the extract below. Jot down brief notes or words to describe how the article makes you feel.

Experience: I was swept away by a flood

'Shocked, tossed and buffeted, I gasped for breath and tried to keep my head above water'

It was after midnight last December and we were driving home from a party. The weather in Devon had been awful. [...] We were in our Ford Ranger pick-up truck, which always felt safe. Paul, my husband, was driving and my seven-year-old son, Silas, was in the back.

[...] One minute we were halfway home and driving up to a familiar bridge, the next there was water rising over the bonnet. Deep floodwater was coursing across from a nearby railway line and surrounding fields, and we were caught in the middle of it. [...]

Water was instantly around my ankles. I reached my hand back and felt it around Silas's, too. Paul climbed out through a window, at which point Silas woke up, confused and disoriented. I managed to pass him through the window to Paul, who was now on the truck's roof. [...]

He grabbed my hood to help, but he was at a precarious angle and I could hear Silas crying, so I told him to let go – Silas needed him. [...] As I saw his empty, outstretched hand, the water took me away. I'm a strong swimmer, but had no option but to shoot down the rapids. Shocked, tossed and buffeted, I gasped for breath and tried to keep my head above water. There was a horrendously loud noise, like a huge wall of bubbles swirling in my ears. Bewildered, I remember saying, 'Oh God, oh God, oh God!' I never expected to die of drowning.

Washed over a garden wall, I joined the River Taw. [...] It was extremely dark but I could just make out trees. As I passed, I reached out and grabbed two branches no bigger than my index finger with a perfect tight grip. Somehow my feet wedged in a firm foothold and I hugged the tree with my knees. One minute longer and I'd have

been sucked beneath a railway bridge. [...]

After nearly 40 minutes, I saw a small spotlight. I started to shout for help. Someone glimpsed my movement and a firefighter tried to talk to me, but I couldn't hear her above the roar of the water.

The light of a helicopter made me out in the tree. [...] My husband, who had been rescued with my son, was nearby with a policewoman. She reassured him that so long as they could hear me, there was hope.

Guided to me by the helicopter, the rescue team managed to steer the boat to my shoulder. Four strong arms lifted me into the boat and I felt sheer relief and utter safety. [...]

My rescuers were volunteers who have since received medals [...]. In the isolation of that tree, I found a strength of character I didn't know I possessed – but I'm still flabbergasted I survived at all.

Activity 2

In this article, Vanessa Glover has described her experience of being swept away by a flood. Remind yourself what a verb is.

1. Complete the table below by listing ten verbs from the extract.

2. Write down the effect of each verb. To do this, think about the meaning of the verb and why it has been used. Think about how the verb contributes to describing Vanessa's overall experience.

Verb	Effect
'tossed'	This makes it sound like she is being thrown around effortlessly in an uncontrolled manner and this emphasizes the intense power of the flood.

Activity 3

1. At the beginning of the text Vanessa Glover tries to convey the fact that she did not know whether she would survive. Write down any phrases which suggest she is feeling terrified and afraid during her ordeal.

2. Vanessa is worried about:

   a) her own safety

   b) the safety of her husband

   c) the safety of her son.

   Copy down two or three phrases about each of these people. Write down two or three words of your own to describe the different feelings she has for each person.

3. Look at the final four paragraphs. Write down any words and phrases that suggest Vanessa's relief.

4. Now you have focused on Vanessa's choice of language, look back at the notes you made in Activity 1 about your initial reactions to the article. Write two paragraphs describing your reaction to her feelings, and quote words and phrases from the article to support your feelings.

Key terms

First person (*I/we*): using first-person narrative allows you to tell a story from the perspective of a character in the text. In non-fiction texts it can be seen as a biased view because it only tells one side of the story

Third person (*he/she/it/they*): using third-person narrative means the story is told from an independent point of view so you can see what all of the characters think and feel. In non-fiction texts it is regarded as an unbiased voice

There are two different types of meaning to look for when reading:

Explicit meaning – to state something openly and exactly. The explicit details in a text are the ones that you can find easily. For example, 'the scarf was soft'.

Implicit meaning – when something is implied but not openly stated. The implicit details in a text require much closer reading so you can find what is implied. For example, 'the scarf clung like a second skin to her neck'.

Activity 4

The writer of the article on page 32 sometimes uses obvious detail to describe the flood. Can you see any explicit or obvious details that are used to describe the following?

- The speed of the flood

- The strength of the flood

- The noise of the water

Now try the activity again and see if you can find any implicit details about these three things. You will need to read the text closely to work out what the writer is implying.

Activity 5

The passage is written in the **first person**. Do you think first person or **third person** is more effective for this type of writing? Why do you think this?

Stretch

Remind yourself of the work on structure on pages 30–31. Think about the order of the events. How does the writer use the structure of the text to build tension?

The Rescue

The following extract documents a similar incident to that of Vanessa Glover's. Read through the information carefully. Use your knowledge of text structure and how a writer can organize their ideas to sequence the information in the correct order.

Thankfully we managed to get phone reception and were able to request assistance.

When we reached Dad he was not in a good way. His ankle was facing the wrong way and he had clearly banged his head as most of his comments were slurred and incoherent.

It was unbelievable how suddenly the cloud levels dropped. The sky turned dark grey almost immediately and the heavy clouds burst open with great force.

The climb began well and conditions were good. We were making excellent time and were having a challenging but enjoyable ascent.

We quickly put on our waterproof clothing but that's when disaster struck. Dad slipped on a piece of slate and tumbled several metres back down the slope.

We left a bright and sunny Llanberis early that morning. Armed with plenty of food, climbing gear and waterproof clothing we felt we were well equipped.

The local Mountain Rescue Team and a rescue helicopter came to our aid. Dad is now recovering at home with his broken ankle in a cast.

You may be asked to produce a narrative piece of writing in your Unit 2 exam. You can use some of the information from the texts you have read to help you to develop your own ideas. The information taken from a reading text can be quoted in your own work, but using it as a springboard for your own creative ideas will help you gain a higher mark. Narrative writing records actions and events from a specific point of view and / or point in time. Narratives can include reports about real events and news stories which enable the reader to form an independent opinion. Narrative texts also include novels, short stories, plays and biographies.

Tip
- Look for any themes within the writing that may help you to deduce the sequence (for example, the weather).
- Look for words like 'finally' or any other time clues in the writing.
- Use your own understanding of a situation to help you to work out a chronological sequence.

Activity 6

Read the following sample exam task:

Write about a difficult journey you have made.

1. Go back through the article written by Vanessa Glover and the sequencing activity about 'The Rescue'. Highlight any words, phrases or ideas that could help you to write about a real journey.

2. Using the ideas you have taken from the texts, write a plan for your own difficult journey. You may want to use the plan below to help you.

Background to the journey ⋯▶ Initial experience ⋯▶ Difficult situation ⋯▶ Ending

9 Understanding the reliability of texts

Learning objectives

- To explore the differences between factual and fictional accounts
- To understand how to question facts
- To consider how to examine the reliability of a text

A writer's style may be influenced by their audience. If they are reporting information for a newspaper article, it is likely that the information will be factual and based on actual events. If a writer is reporting information to entertain or persuade, they may use exaggeration to have an emotional impact on the reader.

A typhoon is a tropical cyclone. You are going to read two texts that describe typhoons. The first text is a news report of Typhoon Haiyan's approach to the Philippines. The second is an extract from a novel called *Typhoon*. The narrator describes the effects of the terrible storm on the ship.

Extract 1

Philippines: thousands evacuated as Typhoon Haiyan strikes

Enormous storm predicted to be largest ever recorded, topping hurricane Camille in 1969, hits north Pacific

Typhoon Haiyan has hit the Philippines with winds of 195mph, with experts saying 'catastrophic damage' will result from what is predicted to be the strongest tropical cyclone to make landfall in recorded history.

Thousands of people have been evacuated and thousands more have fled their homes as the category five storm sent waves as high as 5m ashore [...] overturning powerlines and leaving streets knee-deep in water.

Haiyan – the Philippines' 25th typhoon so far this year – is expected to barrel through the archipelago close to Cebu, the nation's second-largest city and home to around 2.5 million people.

Extract 2

Extract from *Typhoon* by Joseph Conrad

The seas in the dark seemed to rush from all sides to keep her back where she might perish[1]. There was hate in the way she was handled, and a ferocity[2] in the blows that fell. She was like a living creature thrown to the rage of the mob; hustled terribly, struck at, borne up[3], flung down, leaped upon. Captain MacWhirr and Jukes kept hold of each other, deafened by the noise, gagged by the wind; and the great physical tumult[4] beating about their bodies, brought, like an unbridled[5] display of passion, a profound[6] trouble to their souls. One of those wild and appalling shrieks that are heard at times passing mysteriously overhead in the steady roar of a hurricane, swooped, as if borne on wings, upon the ship, and Jukes tried to outscream it.

[1] perish – to die or be destroyed
[2] ferocity – savagery, viciousness, wildness
[3] borne up – from the verb 'to bear', to raise aloft, to support
[4] tumult – a loud noise usually made by a crowd of people
[5] unbridled – not controlled or restrained
[6] profound – very deep or intense

Activity 1

1. Now you have read the extracts, look at the adjectives below and match each one to the correct extract.

    descriptive   factual   fictional   informative

    persuasive   exaggerated   emotional   entertaining

2. What do you think the purpose of each text is?

3. The texts describe the typhoons very differently. List five words or phrases used to describe each typhoon. For example, Conrad: 'like a living creature thrown to the rage of the mob'; the report: 'largest ever recorded'.

> **Tip** Remember, a text can have more than one purpose. Use the adjectives from question 1 to help you.

Stretch

You began to consider how the writers described typhoons differently in question 3, above. Which do you think is the most effective description, and why?

You should think about:

- the words used to describe the typhoons
- which writer makes the typhoon sound most powerful and how they do this
- which you prefer and your reasons for your choice.

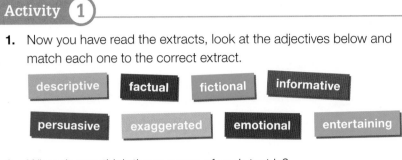

When a writer uses **personification** they represent an idea or an object in human form or give it human characteristics. For example, they may describe a tree as a withered old person with gnarled hands and a stooped posture.

Activity 2

1. Conrad refers to 'she' in the passage. Who or what is he referring to?

2. What is the effect of personifying the typhoon?

Support

Read back through Extract 1 and write down any factual information you can find. How do you know the information is factual?

Key term

Personification: the attribution of a personal nature or human characteristics to something non-human

Both writers mention people in their articles. Conrad mentions two of the sailors on board the ship while Kate Hodal talks about the thousands of people who have been affected by the typhoon. Conrad's narrative gives a clear account of what these two men are experiencing while Hodal uses large numbers (figures) to show the vast number of people who have either been evacuated or have fled.

Activity 3

Write down a word or phrase to describe the people in each of the texts. Write next to it how the information makes you feel.

Support

Read the sample response below which has been written to answer the following exam-style question:

> What do you think and feel about typhoons, as presented in these passages?

I feel that the typhoons seem to swallow up their surroundings, 'The seas in the dark seemed to rush from all sides', suggesting they restrict the movement of everything they cover. The list of verbs used to describe their effect, 'hustled terribly, struck at, borne up, flung down', makes me feel that the typhoon is violent, vindictive and forceful.

Add three or four additional sentences of your own. Make sure you use the following tips:

- Find a piece of evidence that gives you a clear impression or thought about the typhoons.
- Write down what you feel about the typhoons based on the evidence you have selected.
- The question asked you to use both texts so make sure you take information from each one.

Stretch

Use both texts to answer the following exam-style question:

> What do you think and feel about typhoons?
>
> Write two paragraphs in which you use evidence from both texts to support your assertions.

Activity 4

In your own words, write down the differences between factual (non-fiction) and fiction texts. Can you see how they are different?

(10) Effective descriptions

Learning objectives

- To understand the features of effective description
- To draw on descriptive skills to plan and draft a paragraph of writing

Like Conrad's description of the typhoon on page 36, good writers often include some engaging descriptions in their narrative writing. Descriptions are effective when they are generally realistic, detailed and carefully structured. Once the details become unrealistic, the writing loses credibility and becomes unconvincing, unlikely and unsuccessful. When writing effectively, it is essential that you begin with a clear sense of the purpose, audience and the direction of the writing.

Producing an engaging piece of writing can be difficult. Good writers spend time looking around, thinking about things that they find interesting and considering different ways to write about those topics. Some will write about incidents that they have experienced in their own lives, some will exaggerate real events and others will invent details and characters. Whatever their preference, even the best writers will always have some sort of plan before they start, otherwise their writing will lose direction and become vague and uninteresting.

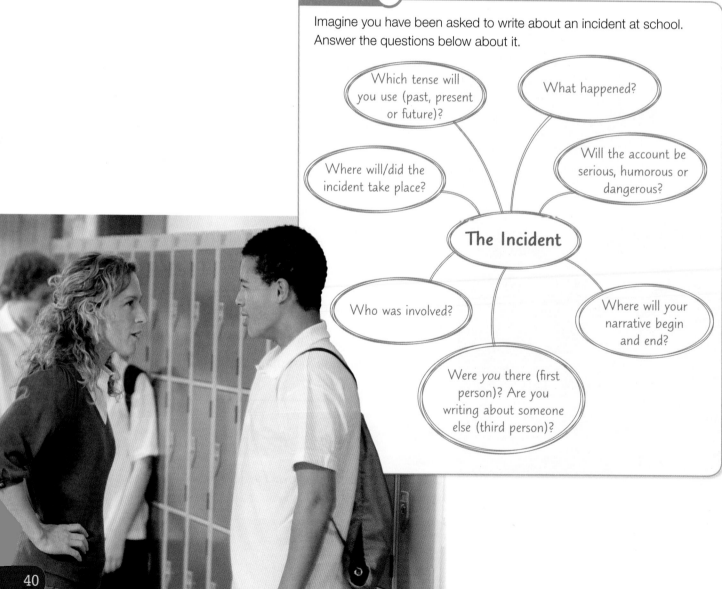

Activity 1

Imagine you have been asked to write about an incident at school. Answer the questions below about it.

- Which tense will you use (past, present or future)?
- What happened?
- Where will/did the incident take place?
- Will the account be serious, humorous or dangerous?

The Incident

- Who was involved?
- Where will your narrative begin and end?
- Were you there (first person)? Are you writing about someone else (third person)?

Activity 2

Using your answers to the questions in Activity 1, select one part of your writing where you think a description of a person, the location or the events would be beneficial.

1. Write down what you are going to describe.
2. Make a list of the main features of that person/place/event.
3. Make a list of possible words you will use in your description.
4. If you wish, make notes on what you intend to write about.

Exam link

Descriptive writing texts describe something in particular (place, person, object or scene) at a specific point in time. In addition to a location-based description, students may be asked to produce a travelogue, a diary extract or an account of an occasion.

Things to avoid

There are a number of key things that you should avoid when describing. Details which are unrealistic or mundane, too general or overly ambitious can spoil your writing.

Activity 3

Working with a partner, read each of the four student examples that follow. Each one has been annotated with questions to help you decide how successful each piece of writing is. Discuss the annotations and decide how each example could be changed. Write your improved versions.

Example 1 – Unrealistic details

1. Does the clothing sound realistic?

The model-like teacher wore a Gucci coat with Armani sunglasses and carried a Louis Vuitton briefcase. Godlike, he strolled into the sunlit and pristine classroom. His Paul Smith shoes tapped noisily on the carpet and echoed like a drum. The rain poured down outside and a heavy wind blew through the tiny cracks in the windows and ruffled his heavily gelled hair.

2. Would shoes tap and echo on a carpet?

3. The classroom was previously sunlit but now it is raining – is this likely?

4. The windows have 'tiny cracks'. Would they allow sufficient wind through to ruffle gelled hair?

41

Example 2 – Mundane details

1. The incident is meant to be at school. Do these details add anything to the story?

I got up that day, had a shower and brushed my teeth. I went to my bedroom and put on my uniform. I went downstairs where my sister had made some toast for me. It was burnt. I threw it away. With a huge sigh I picked up my school bag and headed out of the back door. I closed the gate at the front of my house and headed to the bus stop.

2. The writer uses many simple sentences; what is the effect of this?

3. The vocabulary is straightforward and simple; does it interest you?

Example 3 – Generalized details

1. What was the supply teacher like?

The supply teacher arrived and we entered the classroom. We stood in the room and stared at the ceiling above us while we waited for them to begin. It was going to be another boring lesson, I could tell. One boy put up his hand to ask a question but was ignored. He looked quite flustered and fidgeted. The teacher frowned and droned on about the work we had been set.

2. Who are you talking about? The teacher? Students?

3. Who is he?

4. Describe his movements.

5. Give some extra details. What was the subject? What was their voice like?

Example 4 – Overly ambitious detail

1. Does the writing make complete sense?

The crepuscular light of the evening was created by the soft ambient light cast down from an ancient, rusted streetlight. The sonorous noise created by a congregation of disrespectful chirruping crickets caused a cacophony of sound that ruptured the silence of the otherwise solemn and subdued neighbourhood. An ancient, threadbare, old and weathered tabby cat skulked menacingly around her grateful owner's green door guarding the grizzled and grey-haired pensioner who lurked behind the catflap awaiting the return of her dearly beloved and greatly adored best feline friend.

2. Does it sound fluent?

3. Would you be interested in the rest of this account?

4. The student has overused ambitious vocabulary. Which words would you remove to make this sound more fluent?

Activity 4

1. Look back at the planning work you produced earlier. Are there any details you would like to add to your work? Remember advice from the 'things to avoid' examples.

2. Now write your paragraph.

Progress check

When you have completed your paragraph, read back through your work and complete the following:

- Underline any spellings which you are uncertain about, then check them using a dictionary.

- Read each sentence separately and make sure it makes sense.

- Correct or amend any sections you are unhappy with.

Swap your work with a partner.

- Underline any errors that you can spot.

- Write down what you think will happen next.

- Give two suggestions of details you would add to change or improve their description.

Tip If you are working on a computer and you decide to use the spell check, make sure you check the corrections carefully. For example, many students spell *definitely* incorrectly and when they spell check their work they opt for *defiantly* instead of *definitely*.

Extreme travel

11 How a writer influences the reader

Learning objectives

- To explore the question 'how does a writer…?'

Introduction

Some people choose to visit and explore extreme environments. From hostile, uninhabited islands to jungles, deserts, mountains and vast areas of ice and snow, there are many extreme areas on our planet. These are often dangerous and conditions can be life-threatening.

Students are often asked to think about a writer's techniques and how a writer may try to manipulate feelings. From holiday brochures to charity adverts, writers try to appeal to us and change the way we feel. When we are asked to consider, 'how does the writer…?' we need to think carefully about:

- what the writer actually says
- how the contents might affect the reader
- the writer's method.

Activity 1

Read the extract opposite. The article suggests that this is Sir Ranulph Fiennes' 'greatest challenge to date'.

1. Look at the subheading and write down anything that the writer says here to suggest this is a great challenge.

2. Now look at the rest of the article. How does the writer present the trek as a challenge? Use these questions to help you.

> Do any of the words suggest it is a challenge?

> Does the writer use any numbers or statistics to make the trek sound more challenging?

> What have other people said about the area?

> What will make this adventure difficult?

Activity 2

Now think about each piece of information you have chosen. Can you explain why each of these suggests that the trek will be a challenge?

Support

The writer mentions Captain Robert Falcon Scott and Apsley Cherry-Garrard in the text. Who do you think these people are? Why do you think the writer mentions them?

Stretch

Some of the language is extreme and paints a bleak picture of the expedition. Given the adversity he faces, why do you think Sir Ranulph Fiennes wants to embark on this 'appalling challenge'?

You should look for both explicit and implicit reasons. Remember to support your answer with textual references.

Sir Ranulph Fiennes to attempt record winter Antarctica trek

Veteran explorer describes planned 2,000-mile trek in temperatures as low as −90°C as his greatest challenge to date

The appalling challenge of a six-month 2,000-mile walk across the south pole, in the perpetual darkness of the Antarctic winter when temperatures can plummet to −90°C, proved, perhaps inevitably, irresistible to the veteran explorer Sir Ranulph Fiennes. [...]

Fiennes' hero, Captain Robert Falcon Scott, wrote 'great God, this is an awful place' when he finally reached the south pole a century ago, before freezing and starving to death with his team on the return journey. Apsley Cherry-Garrard called his own trek 'the worst journey in the world'. [...]

Those journeys were made in summer. Nobody before has attempted [...] crossing the pole in winter. In a prepared statement, Fiennes said: 'This will be my greatest challenge to date. We will stretch the limits of human endurance.' [...]

However, in person, at the launch at the Royal Society of The Coldest Journey, Fiennes could not really explain why anyone should contemplate such a venture, still less a man aged 68 who has survived cancer, major heart surgery, and the loss of most of the frozen finger tips on one hand – which he cut off himself with a saw bought specially for the purpose. 'It's what I do,' he said, looking slightly puzzled at the question.

Activity 3

Using all the skills you've looked at in Activities 1 and 2, write two paragraphs to answer the following question:

How does the writer persuade us that this will be a great challenge?

Exam link

The following steps can help you answer 'How...' questions in the exam:

1. When analysing what a writer says, work out who the writer is – in this case it is journalist Maev Kennedy, not Sir Ranulph Fiennes.

2. Look carefully at what the question asks you to do. Are you being asked how the writer persuades you to do something or why you are persuaded that this is a difficult task?

3. Once you understand what you are being asked to look at, start focusing on what the writer says and how they put their ideas together.

4. Pick out words, phrases, techniques or methods and explain how these work in relation to the question.

Picking out words and phrases or stating a technique or method can be meaningless unless you are able to explain how they work in the context of the question. For example:

Where is the emotive language?

The writer uses a wealth of emotive language in the passage.

Why does the writer use emotive language? Why does it suggest the trek is challenging?

12 Effective content

Learning objectives

- To explore how the contents of a text can influence a reader

The content of a text will often have an impact on a reader. Carefully written content can make a reader feel a range of different emotions including guilt, embarrassment, pity or elation. Writers will often construct their content very carefully to manipulate the reader's reactions.

When considering the effect of a text, good readers step back and give an **overview** of what the writer has achieved and how they felt at different points in the text.

Activity 1

Read the following sentences. Look closely at the words used in them. What is the writer trying to make you feel in each example?

The nation weighs up the cost of obesity.

Can you imagine walking for five hours to collect fresh water?

○ **friends of the earth**
see things differently

British teenagers awarded European top spot for charitable donations.

NO ONE SHOULD FACE CANCER ALONE
WE ARE MACMILLAN. CANCER SUPPORT

Renewable energy policies will cost the average household in Britain a total of £400 a year by 2020.

Kira Salak is a woman who completed a solo kayak voyage, travelling 600 miles on the Niger River. This diary extract gives a brief snapshot of a section of her adventure.

Extract from *The Cruelest Journey* by Kira Salak

I wake up with dysentery. Still, I won't give up. Hunched over and faint, I get in my kayak, paddling off down the hottest, most forbidding stretch of the Niger to date. My thermometer reads 112 degrees. The sun burns in a cloudless sky that offers up no hint of a breeze. Great white dunes rise on either side of the river, pulsing with heat waves, little adobe villages half-buried beneath them. [...]

I stick to the very middle of the Niger. An island splits the river, creating a narrow channel on either side. The narrower the river, the more vulnerable I am. There is less

opportunity for escape. All I can do is paddle as hard as I can, following my new guideline: don't get out of the boat—*for anything*. Some men onshore leap into their canoes and chase after me, demanding money. One man comes close enough to hit my kayak with the front of his canoe, nearly grabbing my lead rope with his hand. I'm able to see his face and his wild eyes as I strain to get away. I know one of us will have to give up—him or me. I pace my strokes as if it were a long-distance race, and he falls behind.

Exhausted and nauseous, I squint at the Niger trailing off into the distance, looking as if it's being swallowed by the Sahara. I don't know how much farther I can go on like this.

Activity 2

Summary skills are required to give an effective overview of a text. Re-read the extract from *The Cruelest Journey*. Follow the steps below, which will help you to produce an overview of the content and its effect on a reader's emotions.

1. In no more than 15 words, summarize the main information from each paragraph, for example:

   > The author is unwell and has a fever.
   > The weather is very hot.

2. Write down two or three words to summarize how you feel about the information given in each paragraph.

3. Now look at the information you have written down. Can you give a brief overview of this text in no more than 50 words? Remember to summarize the main information and to reflect on how you feel.

Stretch

In an exam you may be asked to consider how a writer achieves an effect in their text. Look at the exam-style question below and write a brief plan of what you would include in an answer.

How does the author make the reader feel concerned about her health and safety?

To answer this question you should think about:

- what she says to make you feel concerned
- any words or phrases that support your ideas and points
- briefly explaining why you are concerned (*this suggests... this shows...*)
- any techniques used for effect.

Key term

Overview: a general summary, explanation or outline

13 Persuasive writing techniques

Learning objectives

- To understand and explore a range of different techniques that a writer may use for effect

Alongside the language and content of a text, you need to think about the techniques used to create an effect.

Activity 1

1. In pairs, make a list of any persuasive techniques you know. Write down a definition of each of these.

2. Now look at the list you have made and write down why each of these techniques would be effective. (How do they work? What do they do? Why are they persuasive or effective?)

Tip When analysing a text, try to avoid writing vague statements. 'The writer uses short sentences to make me read on' is vague. Always give evidence to support your point or technique, and remember to explain the effect. For example, 'The writer uses short, eye-catching sentences like "It was mesmerizing" to give the reader the clear impression that the events were captivating.'

Read the following text from the travel company Extreme Adventures.

EXTREME ADVENTURES
FANCY AN ADVENTURE YOU'LL NEVER FORGET?

Last year 2.5 million young people took a gap year and we're here to help. If you are looking for exhilarating adventures and remote destinations, then look no further. If you fancy a foray into the Falklands or a trek to Timbuktu, we're here for you. Are you fascinated by cultures, mesmerized by magnificent wildlife or want to sample bizarre local cuisines? We're here to help.

If you're wild about wildlife we can offer a tailor-made camping trip on the Serengeti. If you're nuts about Brazil we can organize an amazing journey that weaves through South America and ends at the breath-taking top of Machu Picchu.

Travel expert Terry Maskell claims our trips, *'allow you to immerse yourself in inspiring journeys and unforgettable adventures'*. With 99.4% customer satisfaction and over 10,000 successful trips each year, you'll be guaranteed an adventure you'll never forget. Our guides are the finest in their fields. We believe we are the best adventure agents around. But don't take our word for it; check out the thousands of reviews from satisfied customers.

Activity 2

Extreme Adventures is trying to persuade potential travellers to embark on one of its adventures.

1. Which emotions does the company appeal to and why?

2. Some persuasive techniques have been listed here. Can you find an example of each of these in the text? Explain why the examples persuade the reader to embark on one of the adventures.

SPAG

Lists – used to show a range of potential reasons.

Quotations – often given by an 'expert' to support a product. An expert's support also suggests reliability/respectability.

Statistics – information that is represented by data or numbers.

Direct appeal – often uses pronouns such as *we, us, our, you.* This appeals to the reader who may feel personally involved in the text and can imagine themselves doing what the text suggests.

Rhetorical questions – questions that are used for dramatic effect, not intended to get an answer. They can suggest there is no alternative course of action.

Proper nouns – give the name of a specific place, person or organization. They are often used to make an argument credible or realistic as they give us something 'real' to think about.

Activity 3

Ben Fogle, a TV presenter and explorer, entered a competition in 1999. The BBC was looking for volunteers to be marooned for a year on an island. Fogle was successful and spent one year on an island in the Outer Hebrides.

Task: A TV company is looking for school leavers and college students who are willing to live on an island for one year with other young people. Successful winners will be filmed as part of the project. You have decided to apply.

1. With a partner, list the qualities and skills that would appeal to the producers of the TV show described in the task above.

2. Make a list of any hobbies, interests and personal characteristics that will make you suitable for the show.

3. Make a list of any persuasive techniques that you will use to attract the attention of the producer.

Tip A lively and interesting response will certainly get you noticed, but careful planning, sensible structure and well-written sentences are also persuasive.

Support

Plan your response. Think carefully about the structure of your work. How will you start and how will you end? What details will you include?

Stretch

Write your application. Try to use a wide range of persuasive techniques and sentence structures. Your application should be at least four paragraphs in length.

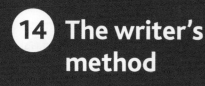

14 The writer's method

Learning objectives

- To explore a range of different methods that can be used by a writer
- To put together the persuasive skills discussed in this unit

The writer's method includes any other ways in which the writer tries to achieve effects. For example, a writer may structure their text in a specific way. They may use comparisons, stark illustrations, anecdotes and so on.

Activity 1

Below is a list of methods writers may use when writing persuasively. Match the methods with their definitions.

Stark illustration   **List/accumulate points**   **Structure**

Dismiss opposing ideas   **Comparison**   **Anecdote**

A A short, often amusing, story about a real person or event. This is an interesting or light-hearted way of giving information.

B Writers can use pictures, graphs, tables, charts or diagrams to support their ideas. Illustrations will make it easy to visualize a point.

C The writer may show a different perspective of two things within a paragraph or even across an entire text. When a writer includes a contrast, readers need to consider why.

D Writers list arguments within a sentence or may choose to build up several across a whole text. Including a range of ideas adds to the strength of an argument.

E Writers organize their arguments to maximize their effect. Texts may be structured in a certain way, for example, to build up tension.

F Writers may be critical of the opposing or counter ideas and use this criticism to further support their own views.

Throughout this unit we have covered a range of different areas that a reader can consider when analysing a text. The real trick is that you need to approach every text individually and think carefully about what each writer is trying to achieve and what/how they have written to achieve it.

Look at the extract opposite, which has been taken from a description of the book *Great Outdoor Adventures*, Bear Grylls' guide to the best outdoor pursuits.

The writer uses a range of questions to…

Picture of well-known adventurer who looks like he is involved in…

A direct appeal 'you' is used throughout and this attracts readers because…

Lists a range of outdoor pursuits, attracting readers because…

Gives a problem … and then a solution … which attracts readers because…

Mentions the writer's name and tells us he is an 'intrepid survival adventurer' because…

| Home | Fiction | Non-Fiction | Authors | About us |

Great Outdoor Adventures by Bear Grylls

Do you long for adventure without being quite sure how to find it? Do you want to sleep under the stars and experience the wonders of the natural world? More of us than ever are spending weekends and holidays climbing mountains, surfing waves or simply walking in the wilderness, as well as indulging in many other more extreme activities. But how can we use our time out in the open to the full? Now, Bear Grylls, one of the most intrepid survival adventurers of our day, shares his years of experience of the world's most extreme terrain to help you get the most from the great outdoors. So, if you've always been intrigued by kite surfing, now's the time to learn how to do it! Find out how to make a tree house or what dangers to watch out for when you're skiing or paragliding. And if you're planning a hike, discover how to navigate across the hills without ever getting lost and what to pack in your rucksack to keep you safe. Whether you're a novice mountaineer looking to graduate from the climbing wall to real rocks or a weekend camper in search of a little more adventure, this is the book for you.

GREAT OUTDOOR ADVENTURES BEAR GRYLLS

THE ULTIMATE GUIDE TO THE BEST OUTDOOR PURSUITS

Gives a range of different activities to…

Subheading gives more information so we know what the book is about.

Activity 2

How does the writer try to attract readers to the book?

1. It is useful to annotate texts so you can have a visual record of your ideas. Some of the extract above has been annotated but the student has not completed their annotations or included arrows to link the annotations with examples. See if you can match up and complete the information for them.

2. Can you find any other techniques in the text that might help to attract readers?

Exam link

When you are preparing to answer a question like this in an exam, ask yourself how the writer is trying to attract you by:

- what they say (language and content)
- the techniques used
- their methods.

When writing up an answer:

- keep referring back to the question
- support every point you make with evidence from the text
- state the effect of every technique used.

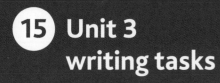

15 Unit 3 writing tasks

Learning objective

- To explore what to do when facing a writing task

Tip Your teacher or an examiner will always give you a clear task when they want you to produce a piece of writing. Your job is to dissect the task and make sure you tackle each element of it in a structured way.

This is the purpose of the writing. You have been asked to persuade and will need to use a range of persuasive techniques to persuade the editor to choose you for the trip.

Key terms

Argumentation writing: argumentation is a form of writing which presents a view of a topic. Students will need to present a range of viewpoints on a given topic. Argumentation texts can include a letter to an editor, a report or an article about a given topic.

Persuasion writing: persuasion is a form of writing which aims to convince a reader of the writer's viewpoint. It may be emotive and will seek to influence a reader's judgement. Persuasive texts can include a speech to a given audience, a letter of protest or a review of a book or film.

In your Unit 3 examination you will be given two writing tasks to complete. One task will be a piece of **argumentation writing** and the other will require you to produce some **persuasion writing**. The task will be linked to the reading materials you have read during the reading section of the exam. You will be given some space to plan your ideas.

You need to have a clear sense of the audience and purpose of the writing but must also consider what you are going to include and how you will structure your work.

Activity 1

Look at the exam-style task below. It has been annotated to help you understand what you need to think about before you plan your work.

Background to the letter – this gives you an idea of what to write about. You can include any information/skills you have to help with the charity work.

You are a student in your local area. Do not assume any other identity for this task as you have been told who you are writing as.

> **Your local newspaper has decided to take three lucky students on an expedition to complete some charity work in a remote African village. Students in your local area have been asked to write a letter to the newspaper persuading the editor to take them on the trip.**
>
> **Write your letter.**

The audience of your writing. You are writing to the editor of the newspaper and need to directly persuade them that you are suitable for the trip.

This is the format of your writing. You have been told to write a letter and need to structure your work appropriately.

Now read the exam-style task below carefully and annotate it like the example above.

> **Your school is keen to raise money to support the newspaper's charity trip to Africa. Write a speech to be given in an assembly at school suggesting how the school can raise money for charity.**
>
> **Write your report.**

Planning your writing

Once you have worked out what you are being asked to write, it is a good idea to plan what you will include. There is no correct way to plan your work; you have to find a method that suits you. Some students like to produce a mind map or spider diagram where they note down all of their ideas (in no particular order). Some students then like to number their ideas so they have an idea of how to structure their work. Other students prefer to produce a logical plan like a flow chart to plan their ideas in a step-by-step process. Try a range of different methods and see which one you prefer.

Why do I want to become involved?

What can I offer to the charity?

What could I do to prepare for the trip?

Any other persuasive techniques/reasons

Competition letter to complete charity work

Why they should choose me — personality, character etc.

What skills/experiences do I have that will be useful in Africa?

Charity speech

Activity 2

Plan your speech from Activity 1 using a flow chart. Think carefully about the order of the information. How will you appeal to your audience? How will you raise the money? Consider any obstacles you may face and how these can be overcome.

Tip Understanding the audience for your writing will help you to adopt the right tone. For example, you may decide to use some humour or light-hearted anecdotes for an audience of your own age.

Activity 3

Read the student's work below:

> Good afternoon, Year 11. I have been asked to talk to you all this afternoon about raising money for the 'Change a Community' scheme we have become involved in. As you know, three students from this school will be sent to a remote African village where they will help to improve a community. I feel there are many ways in which we can raise money for this excellent cause.
>
> Last year the school imposed a sugar ban. To ensure the success of the ban, all of the tasty cakes and treats (that we all love) were sadly removed from our canteen. Mr Jones has promised to lift this ban for one week so we can have a cake sale. I propose a daily cake sale will take place in room 5, every day for a week. Pupils will be free to buy as many cakes as they wish and the proceeds will be put towards the charity.

1. The student who started this speech has been told by their teacher that the contents are not very persuasive. Make a list of what you would do to improve their work.

2. Rewrite their opening paragraph so that the speech appeals to other Year 11 students. Include persuasive techniques to make the work lively and interesting.

3. Swap your work with a partner and see how they have improved the opening. Now reflect on your own work and see what else you could improve.

Does your writing appeal to the audience?

Make a list of the different persuasive techniques you have used and see if there are any others you can add.

Look at the language you have used; can you improve any of it to make it more appealing?

Support

Think about the types of non-fiction writing tasks you have completed in school. Make a list of these different types of writing tasks that you think you could be asked to produce in your exam, for example a formal letter.

Do you know how to structure each of these? If not, make sure you find out any specific features/formats that a writer may use for each type of writing.

Progress check

Having completed the activity on planning a piece of writing and producing an opening paragraph, rate yourself from 1–3 for the following:

1 – I am confident I can do this.

2 – I understand what I am doing.

3 – I need to complete additional work in this area.

- I can read and understand a writing task.
- I understand how to plan a piece of work.
- I can use my plan to structure a piece of work chronologically.
- I can produce a clear opening paragraph.
- I understand how to direct my writing towards a specified audience.
- I can include devices in argumentation and persuasion writing to appeal to a reader.

When you have completed your paragraph, read back through your work and complete the following:

- Underline any spellings which you are uncertain about, then check them using a dictionary.
- Read each sentence separately and make sure it makes sense.
- Correct or amend any sections you are unhappy with.

Swap your work with a partner.

- Underline any errors that you can spot.
- Write down what you think will happen next.
- Give two suggestions of details you would add to change or improve their description.

Assessment

Reading and understanding

Learning objectives

- To identify information within a text
- To practise reading skills

Introduction

In this assessment you will have an opportunity to work through some texts and answer some exam-style questions. Think carefully about the skills you have developed throughout this chapter and make sure you incorporate these into your answers.

Text A

The number of marks alongside each question should give you some indication as to how much information you need to include. Read the text very carefully before you begin answering the questions.

Tip

1. The question has asked for five obstacles so make sure you include *at least* five examples from the text. A list can be written in bullet-point format.

2. Make sure you look for five different groups of people.

3. Remind yourself of the work completed on the writer's perspective. The writer of this leaflet clearly thinks this is an excellent activity as they have used a wealth of positive language to describe the place and the activities.

4. Remind yourself of the work completed on the layout and structure of a text.

Read the text *High Wire Adventure*.

1. List five obstacles that you may face on a high-wire adventure. **[5]**

2. List five groups of people, mentioned in the text, who can enjoy the activities on offer at Aerial Extreme. **[5]**

3. List five examples of positive language used by the writer to persuade people to try out Aerial Extreme. **[5]**

4. Make a list of the different features used by the writer of this text to appeal to a reader. **[5]**

Tip

- If a question asks for a list, remember to write in a bullet-point list.
- When copying points down for a list, do not shorten them so they no longer make sense.
- Check how many marks each question is worth to help you calculate how much detail to include in your answer.

Support

Would you visit Aerial Extreme? If so, why?

Stretch

Think about the lessons on effect. Do you think this is an effective leaflet? Why?

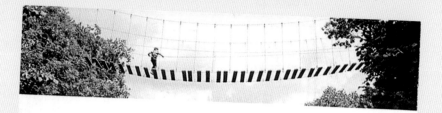

HIGH WIRE ADVENTURE

Aerial Extreme's High Ropes Adventure Courses are an action-packed day out involving a series of challenging obstacles set at varying heights above the ground.

You'll find yourself tackling extreme obstacles such as rope bridges, scramble nets, zip wires, swinging logs and balance beams, plus many more!

JUNIOR ADVENTURE

Once connected by instructors to an overhead safety line, that's it! You remain connected throughout the aerial journey allowing you to concentrate on enjoying yourself.

This means that five out of our six locations are perfect for youngsters as little as six years old!

Plus, no experience or skill is required, so all the kids need is a great sense of adventure.

ADVENTURE PACKAGES

Are you planning a birthday party? Or perhaps an extreme corporate day out?

For an exciting group day out, head for Aerial Extreme and enjoy our challenging and fun obstacles. We can cater for groups from 15 to over 100 but pre-booking is essential.

We've also created a whole host of brilliant birthday, corporate, stag and hen packages aimed at all ages.

PRE-BOOKING IS ESSENTIAL FOR LARGE GROUPS. FOR MORE INFORMATION CALL 0845 652 1736

Text B

High Wire – Staying Safe

The following tips will help you to stay safe while enjoying a day out on our High Wire Adventure.

A

Please make sure you listen carefully and then follow all instructions about what to wear and what to leave behind.

B

When given a harness, please do not secure this until the safety instructor has checked you have put it on properly.

C

Before you are given your equipment you will be given a safety brief.

D

Now you are ready for an adventure. Throughout the session, make sure you follow all instructions. Enjoy yourself.

E

Before being given a harness, please ensure that you have removed everything from your pockets and all valuables or jewellery.

Tip Make sure you don't write down the answer that you have already been given. Check the information carefully to make sure you get the order correct.

5. Text B gives five suggestions of things people should do before enjoying a high-wire adventure. Sequence these suggestions. [3]

The first one has been completed for you:

C Before you are given your equipment you will be given a safety brief.

Text C
Taken from *Zip World*

RESTRICTIONS

	Max	**Min**
Weight	120kg	30kg
Height	2m (6ft 6")	120cm (4ft)
Age	None	7 (Little Zipper) 10 (Big Zipper)*

*NB some children can therefore only ride the Little Zipper.

ZIPPER STATS

	Big Zipper	**Little Zipper**
Max speed	115mph (185kmh)	45mph (73kmh)
Max height above ground	153m (500ft)	22m (72ft)
Length	1600m (approx 1 mile)	450m (1476ft)

A JOURNEY THROUGH TIME

- It was once the largest slate quarry in the world
- The first operations using general anaesthetic (in North Wales) were successfully performed in the quarry hospital
- It was where the first zip lines were built more than 100 years ago to extract rock (these were known as Blondins after the famous tightrope walker)
- Infamously, it is where the longest strike in British industrial history took place
- Today we have the longest zip line in Europe and fastest zip line in the world!

6. What age do you have to be to enjoy the Big Zipper course? **[1]**

7. What is the maximum speed you could travel on the Little Zipper? **[1]**

8. What is the approximate length of the Big Zipper ride? **[1]**

9. What were the first zip lines known as? **[1]**

10. Where can you find the longest zip line in the world? **[1]**

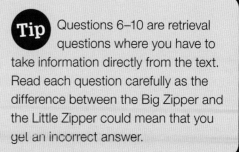

Tip Questions 6–10 are retrieval questions where you have to take information directly from the text. Read each question carefully as the difference between the Big Zipper and the Little Zipper could mean that you get an incorrect answer.

Assessment

Writing

Learning objectives

- To write clearly and adapt your writing to suit the audience and purpose
- To organize your writing and ideas carefully

Introduction

In this assessment you will have an opportunity to plan and write a formal letter. Think carefully about the skills you have developed throughout this chapter and make sure you incorporate these into your writing.

You see the following letter in a local newspaper.

5 Grange Road
Dernham
DH2 3RG

16th September 2015

Dear Editor,

I recently read an article in your newspaper which seemed to celebrate extreme sports. I have to say that I was appalled when I read your views on these ridiculous activities. From bungee jumping to body boarding, skateboarding to skiing, these sports all carry extreme risks.

Young people are, by nature, risk takers. Young people need no encouragement to get involved in ridiculous activities that threaten their lives and worry their families. I appreciate your negative stance on some of the more dangerous sports like tombstoning, but encouraging young people to give free running a go is, to my mind, utterly irresponsible. I am not the type of parent who wishes to wrap my children in cotton wool, but I feel that urging them to try out new and exciting activities will only cause broken bones and broken hearts.

So what's wrong with a game of chess or a stroll around the park? What's wrong with badminton or bowling? I believe…

Task

The letter opposite appeared in a local newspaper. You feel very strongly about the contents of the letter and decide to reply.

Write your letter.

Activity 1

1. Spend five minutes planning your work. If you wish, use the prompts opposite to help you.

2. Go through the letter and underline any of the words or phrases that you wish to discuss or follow up in your response.

3. Make a list of words or phrases to describe how you feel about the letter. This will help you to determine the tone of your letter.

4. Points to consider before you start:

   - Remind yourself of the layout for a formal letter by studying the letter opposite.

   - Who will you address your letter to?

   - What will your opening sentence be?

   - Plan four or five topic sentences that will begin each paragraph in your writing.

5. Share your plan with a partner. Make notes on each other's plans if you can think of any ideas or points that they could include in their work.

6. You now have 30 minutes to write your letter.

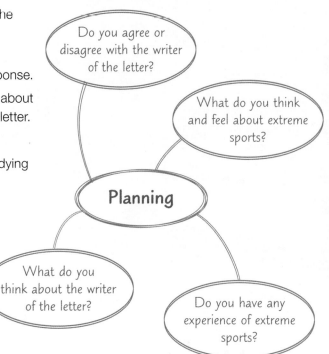

Do you agree or disagree with the writer of the letter?

What do you think and feel about extreme sports?

Planning

What do you think about the writer of the letter?

Do you have any experience of extreme sports?

Support

Try to include a range of sentence types in your work. Use the letter opposite to remind you how to vary your sentences.

Activity 2

Now that you have completed your work, spend two or three minutes reading it to ensure it makes sense.

- Check your work a sentence at a time and make sure each sentence makes complete sense.

- Highlight any spellings you are uncertain about and check them in a dictionary.

- Swap your work with a partner and ask them to annotate your work (in pencil) with suggestions or corrections.

 Tip You can either agree or disagree with the views in the letter, but make sure you have clear, supported opinions.

2 FOOD

In this chapter you will be reading and writing texts that argue,
persuade or instruct, as well as considering description, narration and
exposition. You will be building on some of the skills you have developed
in Chapter 1. You will read and interpret texts that vary in style, content
and the way they present information. This chapter will broaden your
experience of the types of reading text you may encounter in the Unit 2
and 3 exams. You will also find out more about the types of writing you
may be expected to produce and complete activities that will develop
your writing skills in these areas.

'If you can't feed a hundred
people, then feed just one.'
Mother Teresa

'Food has a way of
transporting us back to
the past.' *Homaro Cantu*

'If more of us valued food and
cheer and song above hoarded
gold, it would be a merrier
world.' *J. R. R. Tolkien*

Reading about food

Food is a popular thing to write about and this is probably because it is something that is relevant to everyone. The texts in this chapter are linked by the theme of 'food'. They have been written about food for different purposes and with different audiences in mind. In each of your English Language exams, the texts you read will be grouped thematically, so it is good to get into the habit of looking at different pieces of writing on the same theme. You may be asked to retrieve information from them, you may be asked to show your understanding of what you have read, or you may be asked to synthesize or compare information from more than one text.

Writing about food

In your exams the writing tasks you complete will also be linked by the theme for that paper. In this chapter you will be introduced to different writing tasks and have the opportunity to practise responding to them. This will help you improve and develop your ability to argue, persuade, instruct, describe, narrate and explain in your own writing.

Exploring food

Learning objectives

- To explore the idea and significance of superfoods
- To explore more difficult vocabulary and its effect
- To begin to extract information from a text

Introduction

It is important when you are asked to respond to an idea that you understand what it means. In this case the idea of 'superfoods' is something which has emerged in recent years and is generally connected to foods which are thought to be of significant benefit to a person's health.

Activity 1

Think about what the theme of food means to you:

1. In pairs create a spider diagram of all the different things you associate with food; for example, enjoyment, cultural variety, etc.

2. Join with another pair and compare your findings.

In the dictionary a superfood is defined as: 'A nutrient-rich food considered to be especially beneficial for health and well-being.'

In your exams you will need to be able to read words in context and try to work out what they mean. There may be words that you don't understand in a sentence. There may be words that you think you understand but would struggle to explain. Looking carefully at the words around them will help you to understand their meanings.

Activity 2

1. Write down the definition of a superfood as it appears above. Then underline or highlight it as follows: 'A nutrient-rich food considered to be especially beneficial for health and well-being'.

2. Write a sentence to define each of the highlighted words.

3. Check your definitions in a dictionary and see if they can be improved upon.

4. Rewrite the definition of a superfood but replace each of the highlighted words with a different word or phrase.

There are always different views or ideas that can be presented on the same subject. During the course of this chapter you will see information from various sources that does not always agree. Sometimes you will need to remain objective and 'stand back' from what you are reading in order to be able to take on board different ideas and viewpoints.

Activity 3

The text below has been taken from a longer article about the dangers of labelling some foods as 'superfoods'. Read it carefully, then answer the following questions:

1. Why do nutritionists not recognize the term 'superfoods'?

2. Why does the writer of this article think it is 'dangerous' to think of some foods as 'superfoods'?

3. What does the writer mean by saying that 'the idea of superfoods' has been used to 'sell products'?

4. How does the writer suggest some people may be misusing superfoods?

5. What does the writer mean when s/he says 'use your heads, people'?

So, in theory the whole idea of superfoods sounds brilliant, doesn't it? They're nutritious, they benefit our health and they work against some nasty illnesses. However, in truth the term 'superfood' is not an official label. It is not something that is recognized by all nutritionists or dieticians. They are experts and they know that one food cannot provide all of the nutrients needed by a human body. Setting up a food or a group of foods as the answer to all of our problems is dangerous. There is no quick fix when it comes to healthy and balanced diets. The idea of superfoods is something that has been used, and perhaps overused, to sell products.

Don't get me wrong, there are many foods that have really beneficial properties and can add to a healthy lifestyle but it is the healthy lifestyle itself that is the real key. Too many people are expecting these superfoods to repair damage they have caused to themselves through unhealthy choices. Things like missing sleep, not exercising or eating too many fatty foods cannot be cancelled out by eating a few blueberries. Use your heads, people…

You've read a dictionary definition of the term 'superfoods' and you've read an article where one person argued against labelling foods in such a way. You will be reading more about some of these so-called superfoods in the next part of the chapter so try to remember to keep a sense of balance when reading, however persuasive a text might be. Initially, you will be reading to practise your skills at retrieving and interpreting information.

Superfoods

1 Location of information

Learning objectives

- To practise locating information in a text
- To access a variety of text types

In Chapter 1 you have learned about techniques for locating information quickly such as skimming and scanning. Those skills will be of use to you here as you practise the retrieval of key information. Sometimes questions require you to extract information in a specific way, or from a source that is non-continuous text (see page 17 in Chapter 1). You will be learning more about how to do this.

The way you read the information that surrounds you every day has a significant impact on the decisions you make and the things that you know. For example, you might read a bus timetable app after reading the cinema listings in order to decide what time you need to leave the house to see a film you've been looking forward to. Thinking about the way you read information and the decisions you come to after reading information can help you to understand how and why you get to the right answer.

The extract below is taken from a book called *Healing Foods*. Have a close look at the way in which information is presented here.

A RAINBOW OF PHYTONUTRIENTS

Phytonutrients are the bio-active compounds in plants ("phyto" means plant) that supply their colour and flavour. Although not essential to life in the way that vitamins and minerals are, they support health in a variety of ways.

Antioxidants by colour

COLOUR	PHYTONUTRIENT	BENEFITS	FOUND IN
Green			
	Lutein	Protects eyes; boosts immunity; and supports healthy tissues, skin and blood	Kale, collard greens, cucumber, courgette, peas, avocado, asparagus, green beans
	Chlorophyll	Detoxifying; helps build red blood cells and collagen; boosts energy and well-being	All leafy green vegetables, sprouted grasses, and microalgae
	Indoles	Has anti-cancer properties; supports healthy hormone balance	Brussel sprouts, broccoli, bok choi, cabbage and turnips
Orange/yellow			
	Carotenes (incl. alpha-, beta-, and delta-carotene)	Source of vitamin A; has anti-cancer and heart-protective properties; protects mucous membranes	Orange and yellow fruits and vegetables (peppers, winter squash, carrots, apricots, mangoes, oranges, grapefruit)
	Xanthophylls (incl. zeaxanthin and astaxanthin)	Source of vitamin A; has anti-cancer properties; protects eyes and brain; strengthens the immune system	Red fish (e.g. salmon), eggs, most orange and yellow fruits and vegetables
Red			
	Lycopene	Protects against heart disease, cancer (especially prostate), and vision loss	Fresh and cooked tomatoes, watermelon, goji berries, papaya, and rosehips
	Anthocyanins	Can help reduce the risk of heart disease, cancer and neurodegenerative diseases	Cranberries, strawberries, raspberries, cherries, and red cabbage
Blue/purple			
	Anthocyanins	Fights free radicals; has anti-cancer properties; supports healthy ageing	Blueberries, aubergine, grapes, grape juice, raisins and red wine
	Resveratrol	Has anti-cancer properties; helps balance hormone levels	Grapes, grape juice, red wine, mulberries, and cocoa
White			
	Allyl sulphides	Boosts immunity; has anti-cancer and anti-inflammatory properties	Onions, garlic, scallions, and chives
	Anthoxanthins	Helps lower cholesterol and blood pressure; helps reduce the risk of certain cancers and heart disease	Bananas, cauliflower, mushrooms, onions, parsnips, potatoes, garlic, ginger, and turnips

Activity 1

The following labels have been created to explain what sorts of texts are presented in the extract on page 66. In pairs, discuss the meaning of the following labels. Copy them and cut them out, then place them on the section of text you think they refer to.

This is continuous text →

These are illustrations which emphasize the points being made →

This is non-continuous text →

This is a presentational device to support the points being made →

Activity 2

Discuss in pairs why you made the decisions you did – write a sentence for each label which explains why you put it where you did.

Activity 3

Using your scanning and skimming techniques to locate information, try to answer the following questions:

1. What is a phytonutrient?

2. What does 'phyto' mean?

3. What do antioxidants protect the body from?

4. Name two things that cause free radicals.

5. Name two of the benefits of chlorophyll.

6. What are the phytonutrients called that are found in red foods?

7. Name three sources for anthocyanins.

8. Which phytonutrient protects the eyes and the brain and what food could you eat to include this in your diet?

Below you will find the labels in the correct place with an explanation of why that is the case. Read this carefully.

> This is continuous text – prose writing which is organized into sentences and paragraphs.

A RAINBOW OF PHYTONUTRIENTS

Phytonutrients are the bio-active compounds in plants ("phyto" means plant) that supply their colour and flavour. Although not essential to life in the way that vitamins and minerals are, they support health in a variety of ways.

> This is non-continuous text – information which is presented in a different way to sentences and paragraphs. For example, it could take the form of a list, diagram, graph or chart.

Antioxidants by colour

> These are illustrations which emphasize the points being made – here the information refers to the colour of the food and the supporting picture shows a food of that colour.

COLOUR	PHYTONUTRIENT	BENEFITS	FOUND IN
Green			
	Lutein	Protects eyes; boosts immunity; and supports healthy tissues, skin and blood	Kale, collard greens, cucumber, courgette, peas, avocado, asparagus, green beans
	Chlorophyll	Detoxifying; helps build red blood cells and collagen; boosts energy and well-being	All leafy green vegetables, sprouted grasses, and microalgae
	Indoles	Has anti-cancer properties; supports healthy hormone balance	Brussel sprouts, broccoli, bok choi, cabbage and turnips
Orange/yellow			
	Carotenes (incl. alpha-, beta-, and delta-carotene)	Source of vitamin A; has anti-cancer and heart-protective properties; protects mucous membranes	Orange and yellow fruits and vegetables (peppers, winter squash, carrots, apricots, mangoes, oranges, grapefruit)
	Xanthophylls (incl. zeaxanthin and astaxanthin)	Source of vitamin A; has anti-cancer properties; protects eyes and brain; strengthens the immune system	Red fish (e.g. salmon), eggs, most orange and yellow fruits and vegetables
Red			
	Lycopene	Protects against heart disease, cancer (especially prostate), and vision loss	Fresh and cooked tomatoes, watermelon, goji berries, papaya, and rosehips
	Anthocyanins	Can help reduce the risk of heart disease, cancer and neurodegenerative diseases	Cranberries, strawberries, raspberries, cherries, and red cabbage
Blue/purple			
	Anthocyanins	Fights free radicals; has anti-cancer properties; supports healthy ageing	Blueberries, aubergine, grapes, grape juice, raisins and red wine
	Resveratrol	Has anti-cancer properties; helps balance hormone levels	Grapes, grape juice, red wine, mulberries, and cocoa
White			
	Allyl sulphides	Boosts immunity; has anti-cancer and anti-inflammatory properties	Onions, garlic, scallions, and chives
	Anthoxanthins	Helps lower cholesterol and blood pressure; helps reduce the risk of certain cancers and heart disease	Bananas, cauliflower, mushrooms, onions, parsnips, potatoes, garlic, ginger, and turnips

> This is a presentational device to support the points being made – each section of text which refers to a particular colour is surrounded by a border of that colour to emphasize the point being made.

Activity 4

Read the following extract from a health website. Make a list of ten questions you could ask someone which require them to locate information. Don't forget that sometimes they may need to supply two or three pieces of information to answer a question.

http://medicalinfo.org

MedicalInfo.org

Antioxidants: The facts

What are antioxidants?

Although oxygen is important for the health of your body, when your cells are exposed to oxygen a process called oxidation occurs. During oxidation, the chemicals in the body become altered and become what we call free radicals. Free radicals can also be created by things like smoking, drinking alcohol, exposure to sunlight and polluted air.

Free radicals are responsible for causing chain reactions in the body over time, thereby damaging DNA and cells, sometimes permanently. There is scientific research to show that they also contribute to certain diseases such as heart disease, cancer and diabetes

However, free radicals can be stabilized by antioxidants. Antioxidants are natural substances that are used by your body to stop or reduce the effect of the free radicals and can, to a certain degree, protect your cells and reverse any damage done by oxidation.

Where can you find antioxidants?

Your body will produce a certain amount of antioxidants to fight the free radicals on its own. But this can be helped by eating a healthy diet, in particular by eating fruits and vegetables that have high levels of beta-carotene, selenium, lutein, lycopene and vitamins A, C and E. You can also take supplements which provide antioxidants, but some supplements do not provide a properly balanced selection of vitamins and minerals so you should check with your doctor before using any supplements.

2 Non-continuous texts

Learning objectives

- To develop awareness of non-continuous text types
- To practise locating information from non-continuous texts

In an exam, it is possible that people may think that locating information from a non-continuous text type is easy. This kind of information is often well presented and there is no significant reading to do in order to access it. That does not mean it is easy – careful thought and judgement are required to make sure you have understood exactly what information is provided by the text.

Activity 1

Look carefully at the extracts on pages 71–73. They are all examples of non-continuous texts you may encounter in everyday life. Match each one to its description below.

A Diagram containing information on meat cuts

B Pie chart to show daily intake of calories according to food type

C Data on use of superfoods by restaurants during a specific year

D Guidance from on a healthy eating lifestyle

E Nutritional information on a particular product

F Chart displaying when vegetables are in season

G Information from 'MyFitnessPal' app on someone's daily eating habits

Activity 2

1. Work with a partner. Take it in turns to question each other on information contained in each of the texts. Use at least three different texts.

2. Take the information contained in one of the texts and try to present it in a different way. For example, you could use the data on the use of superfoods in restaurants and present it as a bar graph or pie chart.

Extract 1

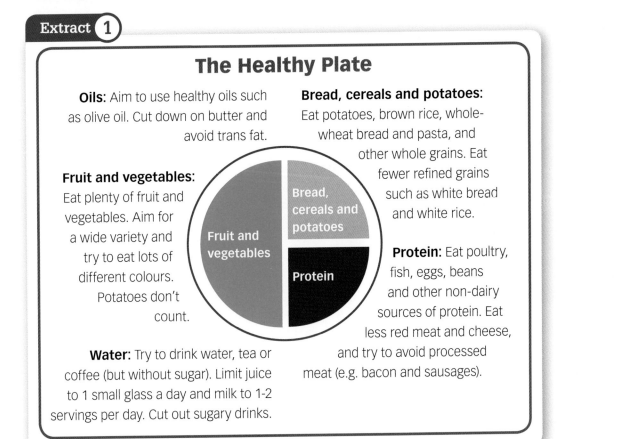

The Healthy Plate

Oils: Aim to use healthy oils such as olive oil. Cut down on butter and avoid trans fat.

Bread, cereals and potatoes: Eat potatoes, brown rice, whole-wheat bread and pasta, and other whole grains. Eat fewer refined grains such as white bread and white rice.

Fruit and vegetables: Eat plenty of fruit and vegetables. Aim for a wide variety and try to eat lots of different colours. Potatoes don't count.

Protein: Eat poultry, fish, eggs, beans and other non-dairy sources of protein. Eat less red meat and cheese, and try to avoid processed meat (e.g. bacon and sausages).

Water: Try to drink water, tea or coffee (but without sugar). Limit juice to 1 small glass a day and milk to 1-2 servings per day. Cut out sugary drinks.

Extract 2

≡	Diary	+
◄	TODAY	►

1,210	1,077	285	792	418
GOAL	FOOD	EXERCISE	NET	REMAINING

Breakfast — 500 cal 🔧

| Strawberries - Raw
1 cup, halves | 49 |
| 1 Scrambled Egg White
1 egg white | 17 |
| Honey
100 g | 304 |
| Nonfat Greek Strained Yogurt
Fage, 1 cup (227 g) | 130 |

Lunch — 577 cal 🔧

| Cilantro Lime Vinaigrette Dressing
Nordstom Cafe, 2 TBSP | 180 |
| Beans - Black, cooked, boiled, with salt
1 cup | 227 |
| 100% Apple Juice
Old Orchard, 8 oz | 120 |
| Guacamole Medium | 50 |

Extract 3

Top superfoods offered at restaurants	
Rate of appearance on menus in 2012	
Superfood	% menu penetration
Avocado	35.6%
Olive oil	30.1%
Walnuts	23.6%
Blueberries	20%
Sweet potato	18.6%
Oatmeal	15.7%
Pomegranate	12.7%
Pumpkin	10.7%
Beets	8.5%
Brown rice	8.3%
Source: Datassential Menu Trends	

Extract 4

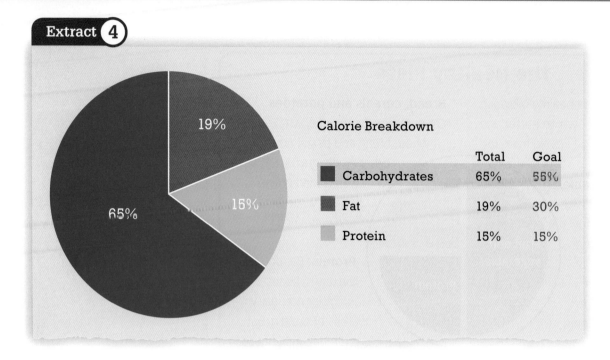

Calorie Breakdown

		Total	Goal
■ Carbohydrates		65%	55%
■ Fat		19%	30%
■ Protein		15%	15%

Extract 5

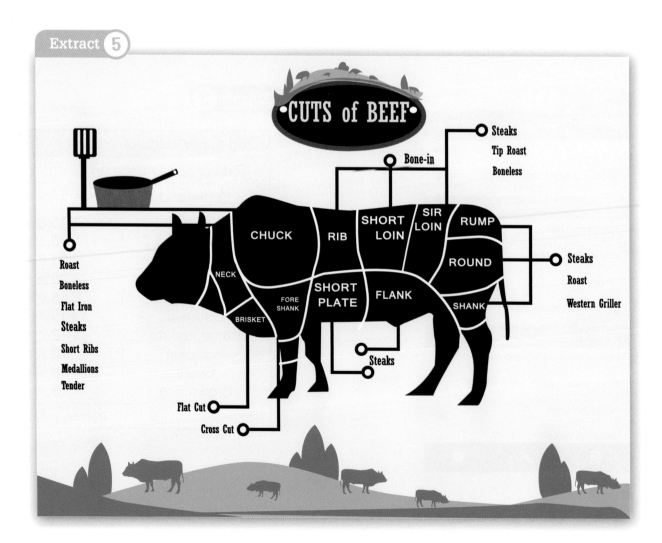

Extract 6

Each grilled burger (94 g) contains

Energy 924 kJ 220 kcal	Fat 13 g	Saturates 5.9 g	Sugars 0.8 g	Salt 0.7 g
11%	19%	30%	<1%	12%

of an adult's reference intake

Typical values (as sold) per 100 g: Energy 966 kJ/ 230 kcal

Extract 7

vegetables
when are they in season?

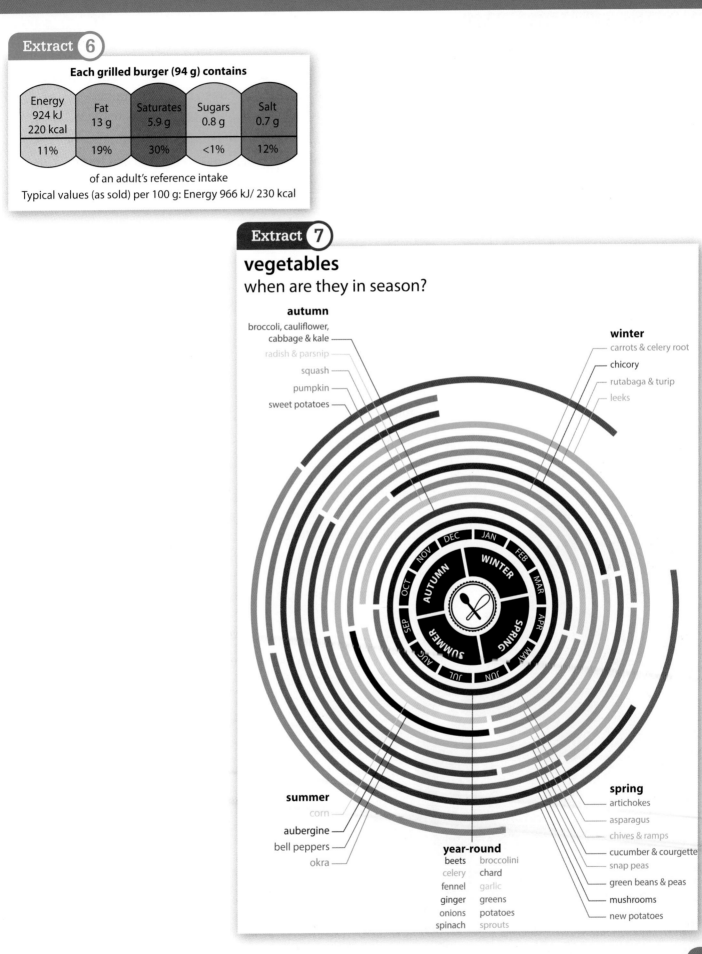

autumn
broccoli, cauliflower, cabbage & kale
radish & parsnip
squash
pumpkin
sweet potatoes

winter
carrots & celery root
chicory
rutabaga & turip
leeks

summer
corn
aubergine
bell peppers
okra

year-round
beets	broccolini
celery	chard
fennel	garlic
ginger	greens
onions	potatoes
spinach	sprouts

spring
artichokes
asparagus
chives & ramps
cucumber & courgette
snap peas
green beans & peas
mushrooms
new potatoes

3 Instructional writing

Learning objectives

- To understand what instructional writing is
- To explore techniques for use in instructional writing

Key terms

Imperative: an imperative verb **SPAG** is used in a sentence where a writer or speaker is giving an order or telling someone to do something. For example:

Go home!

You *take* the dog for a walk.

Use your time wisely.

Writing to instruct involves giving your reader a series of directions on what to do. Precise and clear thinking and careful language choice are required in this type of writing to make sure that no mistakes are made. This type of writing tends to be quite straightforward in expression. Don't make the mistake of thinking that means it is simple – an eye for detail is very important here.

When writing to instruct you are likely to need to use **imperatives** or commands. This is in order to make it absolutely clear what you want someone to do and remove any of the doubt which may creep in with vaguer statements.

Activity 1

Look at the list of vocabulary below. Choose five verbs and write a sentence for each using them as an imperative: **SPAG**

paint	explain	give
shout	take	open
purchase	whip	sort
run	put	improve
blend	locate	decide

In instructive writing structure and organization are very important. For example, if you were writing a first-aid guide on how to treat someone who has suffered a minor burn in the kitchen, the order in which you arrange your writing is crucial. The first thing you might need to tell your reader is what items they may need to treat the burn, so that they are able to assemble these before following your instructions.

An example of instructive writing which is often used in relation to food is a recipe. Take a look at the following recipe taken from a book called *The Superfood Diet*:

Superfoods Toad in the Hole

220 kcal/5.5g fat
serves 8

Spelt flour means an altogether healthier take on a hearty favourite that would otherwise be off-limits.

8 low-fat pork sausages
225g white spelt flour
½ teaspoon turmeric
4 eggs
1 tablespoon wholegrain mustard
250ml semi-skimmed milk
freshly ground black pepper and sea salt, to taste
2 tablespoons chopped fresh sage leaves

Preheat the oven to 220°C/fan 200°C/Gas Mark 7. Line a roasting tin (approximately 30 × 25 cm) with greaseproof paper and arrange the sausages in the tin.

Bake the sausages in the centre of the oven for 10 minutes. Increase the oven temperature to the maximum setting and continue baking for another 5 minutes.

In a large bowl, whisk together the flour, turmeric, eggs, mustard and half the milk until a smooth, thin batter is achieved. Add seasoning to taste.

Remove the sausages from the oven. Ladle over the batter and sprinkle on the sage. Return the tin to the oven and reduce the temperature back to 220°C/fan 200°C/Gas Mark 7. Bake for 30–35 minutes, or until the mixture is risen and brown.

Activity 2

1. In pairs, make a list of all the imperative verbs used in this recipe.

2. Can you change any of these verbs for another which still produces the same effect?

3. Can you explain why the instructions might have become less clear when you changed the imperative verbs?

Activity 3

1. Using the chart below for guidance, write a complete recipe for a meal you can cook.

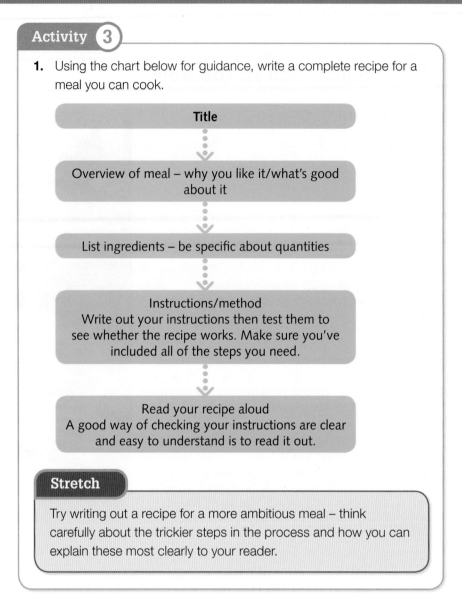

Title

Overview of meal – why you like it/what's good about it

List ingredients – be specific about quantities

Instructions/method
Write out your instructions then test them to see whether the recipe works. Make sure you've included all of the steps you need.

Read your recipe aloud
A good way of checking your instructions are clear and easy to understand is to read it out.

Stretch

Try writing out a recipe for a more ambitious meal – think carefully about the trickier steps in the process and how you can explain these most clearly to your reader.

Being able to proofread work to spot errors is very important and a section of your Unit 2 exam will be devoted to this.

Activity 4

Using the recipes that you created earlier, swap with a partner and proofread each other's work in the same way by identifying and correcting any errors.

Activity 5

Read the following recipe and see if you can find and correct six errors that have been made by the writer.

Homemaid cheese and tomato pizza

1 teaspoon of olive oil
200g plain flour
1 pack dried yeast
1 teaspoon sugar
125ml warm water
50ml tomato puree
100g grayted cheese

1. Heat oven to 240°C/220°C fan/Gas 8. Rub a large baking tray with oil.

2. Stir the flower, yeast and sugar together in a bowl, then mix in the water.

3. Knead until smooth, then rolling out on the oven tray.

4. Spread tomato puree over the dough but don't go quite to the edge.

5. Scatter the cheese over the top.

6. Bake for 15 minute's.

7. Surve with a salad or beans.

(4) Expository writing

Learning objectives

- To understand what expository writing is
- To explore techniques for use in expository writing

Tip When conducting research you can record any really useful quotations word-for-word. Always note down who said it and where it came from, though. Be careful about copying whole chunks of material when writing up your essay. This is plagiarism (pretending someone else's ideas are your own) and does not show your own writing skill. When using source material, rewrite ideas in your own words and show your own thoughts. If you are quoting directly from someone else, you must use correct punctuation to demonstrate that.

An exposition provides a simple explanation of concepts or ideas. It attempts to explain or describe something in a way that helps the reader understand what they are reading. A summary of events in a brochure and a newspaper article which records something that has taken place are both examples of expository writing.

Textbooks and reference books also contain expository writing as they try to help a reader understand the information presented in them. Indeed, much of this book contains expository writing. Sometimes diagrams feature as part of an exposition to visually support understanding (for example, a graph or a flow chart). You may be asked to produce an expository essay if you are asked to present your knowledge or ideas about a particular subject.

To write an expository essay you will need to:

1. research the topic you are to discuss
2. plan your response carefully
3. introduce your topic with clarity and purpose
4. have a clear idea of what you want to say/the direction your essay will take
5. make sure you can develop and give examples for the points you make
6. offer some connections between points
7. conclude with purpose – return to the main concept of your essay, as supported by the points you have made.

Activity 1

You are going to plan an answer to the following exam-style question:

> **Write an essay about the importance of superfoods to a healthy lifestyle.**

Before you do this you will need to do some research. The preceding pages of this chapter may be useful to you, but you should also do some of your own reading (you may find it helpful to use the library and/or the Internet at this point). Make some notes about things you think will be useful as you read, and try to come to a decision about whether superfoods are important to a healthy lifestyle or not.

Activity 2

Look carefully at the guidance below on how to plan an expository essay. Use this to help you write a plan for your own essay.

This is a planning template for expository writing:

> Introductory paragraph – make clear your aims here – what is the purpose of this essay? (HINT: underlining key words in the exam question will make sure you have clearly understood this.)
> Try to find some way of engaging your reader – you might provide them with some interesting evidence or a relevant fact to grab their attention.

> Main argument – first section/paragraph
> Write down your first argument – what is it?
> How are you going to explain and support it? You will need evidence and logical explanation.
> Do you need to offer a concluding statement about what you have said before you move on? Can you link it to your next paragraph?

> Main argument – second section/paragraph
> Write down your next argument – what is it?
> How are you going to explain and support it? You will need evidence and logical explanation.
> Do you need to offer a concluding statement about what you have said before you move on? Can you link it to your next paragraph?

> Main argument – third section/paragraph
> Write down your next argument – what is it?
> How are you going to explain and support it? You will need evidence and logical explanation.
> Do you need to offer a concluding statement about what you have said before you move on?

> Conclusion – this is your chance to make a final statement based on all that you have written. You should repeat your initial argument (using different words if you can) then summarize the arguments you have put forward. End with a final statement on the topic – try to keep your reader interested and encourage them to continue thinking about what you have discussed.

Progress check

1. Ask a partner to read your plan and think about whether you have done what the planning template requires. Ask them to note down three areas of your plan that could be improved. For example, is there something that doesn't work? Is more detail required anywhere? Does the structure of your argument make sense?

2. Amend your plan in light of your partner's comments. Write a paragraph explaining what you have done to improve your work and why this will work more effectively.

Food in fiction

5 Revealing details

Learning objectives

- To investigate further the implicit ways writers reveal information
- To develop personal and descriptive detail in narrative writing

Introduction

A lot of the information we receive as we read comes through implicit ideas. In Chapter 1 you found implicit details in a non-fiction text. You can use the same skills when identifying implicit information in fictional writing. When your teachers have talked to you about your own creative writing you may have heard them say, 'Show me, don't tell me.' This is what good writers try to do – they show you a picture of a character or a setting through their words. You must then infer what they mean from that picture. A writer sows the seeds of an idea in your head, giving you clues and hints about the direction they would like you to take, but ultimately it is up to you to make your mind up about it.

Read the following extract from *A Christmas Carol* by Charles Dickens:

Extract from *A Christmas Carol* by Charles Dickens

There never was such a goose. Bob said he didn't believe there ever was such a goose cooked. Its tenderness and flavour, size and cheapness, were the themes of universal admiration. Eked out by apple-sauce and mashed potatoes, it was a sufficient dinner for the whole family; indeed, as Mrs Cratchit said with great delight (surveying one small atom of a bone upon the dish), they hadn't ate it all at last. Yet every one had had enough, and the youngest Cratchits in particular, were steeped in sage and onion to the eyebrows. But now, the plates being changed by Miss Belinda, Mrs Cratchit left the room alone – too nervous to bear witnesses – to take the pudding up and bring it in.

Activity 1

1. This scene describes a Christmas meal. Read the extract again, thinking carefully about how you visualize the meal and what it is that leads you to those conclusions.

2. Copy and complete the table below. Some of the boxes have been filled in already as examples, but you could add to these with thoughts of your own.

Evidence	Initial thoughts	Development of ideas
There never was such a goose	it's a big goose	*They've never seen a goose like this before. This is the best goose they've ever had at Christmas.*
Its tenderness and flavour, size and cheapness	it was tasty and reasonably priced	*Why mention the cost unless it is important? Perhaps the point is that this was a big, tender and flavourful goose for the price*
universal admiration	everyone admired the goose	
Eked out by apple-sauce and mashed potatoes		
it was a sufficient dinner for the whole family	'sufficient' suggests 'just enough'	*This gives the impression that they are full from their Christmas dinner and perhaps they are not used to 'sufficient' dinner. We don't get the idea of overeating and feasting that many descriptions of Christmas dinners would contain.*
they hadn't ate it all at last		
every one had had enough		
the youngest Cratchits in particular, were steeped in sage and onion to the eyebrows		
Mrs Cratchit left the room alone – too nervous to bear witnesses – to take the pudding up and bring it in		

Tip When writing about implicit meaning you will usually be putting forward your ideas as a suggestion about what the writer might mean. Below are some useful words and phrases that you could use as part of an answer to show that you are engaging with implied meaning.

this shows…

this suggests…

this implies…

this gives the impression that…

perhaps the writer…

the writer may be inferring that…

Some of the best narratives and descriptions written by students come from direct experience. Using yourself as a character in a story makes sense because you know a lot about yourself and will find it easy to write convincingly and in detail on the subject. Also, your writing will feel more authentic and realistic because you will be writing about things that have happened (or could happen) to you in places you are very familiar with. The other characters in your story are likely to be based on people you know well, which will add to the success of your story.

Activity 2

Imagine you are writing an account of something that has happened to you. Before you get into the action/plot you will need to give the reader some information about yourself. It's likely that you will want the reader to empathize with you and be on your side through the main events of the story. Make a list of the key information a reader will need to know about you. For example, there may be details to do with your appearance, your personality or your relationships with family and friends.

Activity 3

You will be able to explicitly tell the reader some of the information on the list you have just created. However, it would not be interesting or engaging if you took that approach with all of the information. Take three of the details from your list and write at least two or three sentences for each that would implicitly convey the information to the reader. Use real experiences to help you where you can.

For example:

I am quite shy around people I don't know might become:

I stood back not quite knowing what to say. Although Mrs Rose smiled encouragingly, this was the first time I'd met her and I could do little more than shuffle my feet and look at the floor. Glancing up nervously, I gave a tentative half-smile and quietly cleared my throat.

Key term

Figurative language: a word or phrase that shouldn't be taken literally, for example, 'the drying clothes waved like proud flags'. Figurative language calls on the reader to use their imagination to complete the writer's meaning and almost always takes the form of either metaphors or similes.

Activity 4

The following extract provides a lot of explicit information about a person. It is quite straightforward but would not interest a reader. Using this as a starting point, rewrite it as if this person appears as a character in a story. Make sure much more of this information is revealed implicitly. In other words, show the reader some of the details – perhaps using **figurative language** – without directly telling them.

The student

Jenny was a greedy child. She always ate more than her fair share at dinner time. She ate her dinner more quickly than anyone else and was always the first to have second helpings. She sneaked biscuits from the jar when no one was looking. She also kept a supply of crisps and sweets hidden in her bedroom. Jenny took food from her friends' lunchboxes at school and never shared her own food.

Activity 5

Write a short character description of someone you know well, paying attention to both explicit and implicit information.

Activity 6

1. Ask a partner to read your work and then complete the first two columns of the table below with five things that they learn about your character. Two of these details must be implicitly learned.

Details discovered about the character	Is it explicitly or implicitly presented?	What else could the writer have included here?	Your response
1.			
2.			
3.			
4.			
5.			

2. Next, ask your partner to complete the third column of the table to help you improve your writing. They should think about how you could make your ideas clearer or provide more detail.

3. In the fourth column of the table you should indicate which of their comments you find helpful and why. Explain how you would use them to help you improve your writing.

6 Giving explanation

Learning objectives

- To consider the meaning of the word 'explain'
- To think about how to explain in an answer

You will encounter questions in your exams that require you to explain yourself. Sometimes you will be told to explain and sometimes you will be asked to choose a correct explanation as part of a multiple choice question. At other times, though, you will need to work out that an explanation is required. Does the question tell you to use evidence from the text to support your answer? If so, that will require an explanation. Sometimes just the fact that a number of lines have been set out for you to write your answer on can be a suggestion that an explanation will be needed.

What is an explanation? The dictionary defines it in two ways:

1. A statement or account that makes something clear.

   For example, 'Parmesan is the cheese that is used in pesto sauce.'

2. A reason or justification given for an action or belief.

   For example, 'I try to eat healthily but it's fine to have the odd treat because above all we should have balance and variety in our diet.'

When you have to explain yourself in writing it is important to justify or give reasons to make it absolutely clear why you think something.

Activity 1

When writing an explanation you will be giving reasons to support whatever point you are making. In pairs make a list of any words or phrases you can think of that you might use when trying to explain something, such as 'This is because' or 'This suggests'.

You are going to be looking at examples of fictional writing which describe how food may be considered in the future or in an alternative reality.

The following extract from *The Hunger Games: Catching Fire* by Suzanne Collins is set at the scene of a banquet. This book is narrated by its central character, a girl called Katniss. Read it carefully:

Extract from *The Hunger Games* by Suzanne Collins

But the real star of the evening is the food. Tables laden with delicacies line the walls. Everything you can think of, and things you have never dreamed of, lie in wait. Whole roasted cows and pigs and goats still turning on spits. Huge platters of fowl stuffed with savoury fruits and nuts. Ocean creatures drizzled in sauces or begging to be dipped in spicy concoctions. Countless cheeses, breads, vegetables, sweets, waterfalls of wine and streams of spirits that flicker with flames.

My appetite has returned with my desire to fight back. After weeks of feeling too worried to eat, I'm famished.

'I want to taste everything in the room,' I tell Peeta. [...]

'Then you'd better pace yourself,' he says.

'OK, no more than one bite of each dish,' I say. My resolve is almost immediately broken at the first table, which has twenty or so soups, when I encounter a creamy pumpkin brew sprinkled with slivered nuts and tiny black seeds. 'I could just eat this all night!' I exclaim. But I don't. I weaken again at a clear green broth that I can only describe as tasting like spring time, and again when I try a frothy pink soup dotted with raspberries. [...]

Every table presents new temptations, and even on my restricted one-taste-per-dish regimen, I begin filling up quickly. I pick up a small roasted bird, bite into it, and my tongue floods with orange sauce. Delicious. But I make Peeta eat the remainder because I want to keep tasting things, and the idea of throwing away food, as I see so many people doing so casually, is abhorrent to me. After about ten tables I'm stuffed, and we've only sampled a small number of the dishes available.

Just then my prep team descends on us. They're nearly incoherent between the alcohol they've consumed and their ecstasy at being at such a grand affair.

'Why aren't you eating?' asks Octavia.

'I have been, but I can't hold another bite,' I say. They all laugh as if that's the silliest thing they've ever heard.

'No one lets that stop them!' says Flavius. They lead us over to a table that holds tiny stemmed wineglasses filled with clear liquid. 'Drink this!'

Peeta picks one up to take a sip and they lose it.

'Not here!' shrieks Octavia.

'You have to do it in there,' says Venia, pointing to doors that lead to the toilets. 'Or you'll get it all over the floor!'

Peeta looks at the glass again and puts it together. 'You mean this will make me puke?'

My prep team laugh hysterically. 'Of course, so you can keep eating,' says Octavia. 'I've been in there twice already. Everyone does it, or else how would you have any fun at a feast?'

I'm speechless, staring at the pretty little glasses and all they imply. Peeta sets his back on the table with such precision you'd think it might detonate. 'Come on, Katniss, let's dance.'

Activity 2

Re-read the extract then answer the following exam-style questions, paying careful attention to the explanation in your answers.

1. What does Katniss mean when she says, 'But the real star of the evening is the food'?

2. How does the writer create an impression of lavish abundance in the opening paragraph?

3. In line 16 Katniss describes 'a creamy pumpkin brew sprinkled with slivered nuts and tiny black seeds'.

   Select one explanation from the list below which best describes the meaning of 'slivered':

   i. broken into thin narrowed pieces

   ii. slipping or sliding across a surface

   iii. a shiny grey colour

   iv. a miniature version of something.

4. Katniss describes 'casually' throwing away food as 'abhorrent'. Explain what she means.

5. Explain what the clear liquid is used for.

6. Explain what Katniss's thoughts and feelings are upon learning what the clear liquid is for. Support your answer with evidence from the text.

What to do if you don't understand what a question is asking you

Look at question 2 in Activity 2. Do you know what the words 'lavish abundance' mean? If you don't, look carefully at the text – what sort of scene is this describing? Can you work out what the question is asking from what is being described by the content?

Lavish means that something is rich or extravagant. Abundance means a very large quantity of something. Together they suggest a very large quantity of rich or extravagant items.

Activity 3

Sometimes you may be asked to explain your own thoughts and feelings – your reaction to something you have read. Using evidence from the text to support your answer, explain your thoughts and feelings as you read the passage.

Read the following extract from *Oryx and Crake* by Margaret Atwood. This is discussing 'ChickieNobs', an imaginative idea of how genetically modified food of the future could be produced.

Extract from *Oryx and Crake* by Margaret Atwood

What they were looking at was a large bulblike object that seemed to be covered with stippled whitish-yellow skin. Out of it came twenty thick fleshy tubes, and at the end of each tube another bulb was growing.

'What the hell is it?' said Jimmy.

'Those are chickens,' said Crake. 'Chicken parts. Just the breasts, on this one. They've got ones that specialize in drumsticks too, twelve to a growth unit.'

'But there aren't any heads…'

'That's the head in the middle,' said the woman. 'There's a mouth opening at the top, they dump nutrients in there. No eyes or beak or anything, they don't need those.'

Activity 4

1. Re-read the extract above carefully and then try to draw and label a diagram of what you imagine the 'ChickieNob' would look like.

2. Write a paragraph explaining what you know about 'ChickieNobs'.

3. What do you think about this idea of food in the future? Advances in genetic modification may make something similar a possibility at some point. Write down three initial thoughts you have about this – be careful to explain the reasons behind your thoughts.

Now read the following extract from the science fiction novel *The Restaurant at the End of the Universe* by Douglas Adams.

Extract from *The Restaurant at the End of the Universe* by Douglas Adams

A large dairy animal approaches Zaphod Beeblebrox's table, a large fat meaty quadruped of the bovine type with large watery eyes, small horns and what might almost have been an ingratiating smile on its lips.

'Good evening,' it lowed and sat back heavily on its haunches, 'I am the main Dish of the Day. May I interest you in parts of my body?' It harrumphed and gurgled a bit, wriggled its hind quarters into a more comfortable position and gazed peacefully at them.

Its gaze was met by looks of startled bewilderment from Arthur and Trillian, a resigned shrug from Ford Prefect and naked hunger from Zaphod Beeblebrox.

'Something off the shoulder, perhaps,' suggested the animal, 'braised in a white wine sauce?'

'Er, *your* shoulder?' said Arthur in a horrified whisper.

'But naturally my shoulder, sir,' mooed the animal contentedly, 'nobody else's is mine to offer.'

Zaphod leapt to his feet and started prodding and feeling the animal's shoulder appreciatively.

'Or the rump is very good,' murmured the animal. 'I've been exercising it and eating plenty of grain, so there's a lot of good meat there.' It gave a mellow grunt, gurgled again and started to chew the cud. It swallowed the cud again.

'Or a casserole of me, perhaps?' it added.

'You mean this animal actually wants us to eat it?' whispered Trillian to Ford.

'Me?' said Ford, with a glazed look in his eyes. 'I don't mean anything.'

'That's absolutely horrible,' exclaimed Arthur, 'the most revolting thing I've ever heard.'

'What's the problem, Earthman?' said Zaphod, now transfering his attention to the animal's enormous rump.

'I just don't want to eat an animal that's standing there inviting me to,' said Arthur, 'it's heartless.'

'Better than eating an animal that doesn't want to be eaten,' said Zaphod.

You might be asked the following question about the extract on page 87:

> **Arthur and Zaphod react in completely different ways to the Dish of the Day. Explain their reactions using evidence to support your answer.**

To answer this question you need to use evidence from the text to explain the following:

1. how Arthur reacts to the Dish of the Day

2. how Zaphod reacts to the Dish of the Day.

The evidence you use might be explicit or implicit.

Activity 5

1. Copy out and complete the following table to provide you with material you can use to answer this question:

Arthur		Zaphod	
Evidence	**What this suggests**	**Evidence**	**What this suggests**
'Its gaze was met by looks of startled bewilderment from Arthur'	He is shocked and confused by what the Dish of the Day has said.	'… and naked hunger from Zaphod Beeblebrox'	Zaphod does not try to mask his hunger – it is 'naked' and there for everyone to see.
'Er, your shoulder?' said Arthur in a horrified whisper		'Zaphod leapt to his feet and started prodding… the animal's shoulder appreciatively'	

2. Use the table to help you write an answer to the exam-style question opposite.

Stretch

One way to answer the question opposite is by dealing with Arthur's and then Zaphod's reactions in turn. While this would provide all of the information that is needed, it would not provide the most concise answer or be the most efficient use of time. Many of the points that can be made about the two characters are in relation to the same idea, and it may be more efficient to deal with them together.

Here is the start of a student's answer. Try to complete it in the same style:

Arthur and Zaphod's initial reactions to the Dish of the Day are very different. Arthur is shocked and confused by the prospect of eating the animal who is addressing them, meeting his 'gaze' with a look of 'startled bewilderment'. Conversely for Zaphod this seems an everyday occurrence proved by the 'naked' and very obvious 'hunger' that the appearance of the Dish of the Day produces.

Progress check

Exchange your answers to the exam-style question with a partner. Read each other's work carefully and highlight two places where you think the answer would benefit from clearer explanation. Rewrite those sections of your own work to address this.

Eating out

7 Synthesizing information

Learning objectives

- To understand the term 'synthesis'
- To explore how to synthesize information from more than one text

Key term

Synthesize: to form something by bringing together information from different sources

In the exams you will read a number of different texts which are thematically linked. You may well be asked to **synthesize** the information or data you have read from two or more texts. This means that after reading the texts carefully, you must combine the information you have found to answer the question you have been set.

Activity 1

Look carefully at the texts that follow. In pairs answer the following questions:

1. What is the main thematic focus of each of these texts?

2. What is the individual purpose of each text?

Activity 2

Copy out and complete the following table to show what you find out about the Food Hygiene Rating scheme from the three texts:

	Extract 1 – 'Don't Eat Here'	Extract 2 – 'What to Look for When Eating Out'	Extract 3 – 'More than 400 food outlets rated sub-standard...'
Who operates the Food Hygiene Rating scheme?	Food Standards Agency		Food Standards Agency
Who runs the scheme in partnership with them?			
What does the text tell you about food hygiene?			
What is the Food Hygiene Rating Score out of?			
Where can you find out about the PASS mark?			
Who is eligible for a Food Hygiene Rating?			
How can food businesses let you know their score?			
Where can customers find more information on this scheme?			
What should a customer do if they doubt the hygiene standards of a place?			

Extract **1**

Extract **2**

What to Look for When Eating Out

Here are some of the tell-tale clues you can look out for when choosing somewhere to eat out or buy a take away.

Positive signs
- Clean public areas
- Staff wash their hands regularly between different tasks (like handling raw meat and then ready-to-eat-foods or cleaning and clearing tables and then going on to serve ready-to-eat foods)
- Hot food is served hot and cooked right the way through, unless it has been ordered otherwise
- Cold food is served cold
- On a carvery, salad bar or delicatessen counter, dishes of food are not just topped-up, but the whole dish changed
- If you can see into the kitchen as doors open or behind servery areas they are clean and reasonably tidy
- Clean and smart looking staff who are dressed for the job

Warning signs
- Overflowing waste bins and dirty or untidy rubbish areas
- Dirty looking staff, with dirty hands or fingernails or dirty habits
- Staff wearing dirty overalls, uniforms or aprons and long hair that is not tied back
- Dirty toilets and wash-hand basins and a lack of soap and toilet paper
- Dirty tables, cutlery, crockery and glassware
- Hair, insects or other matter in the food
- Food on sale past its 'use-by' date
- Raw foods (especially raw meat) stored right next to cooked foods or the same utensils used for both

It's best to base your judgement on a few of the above clues, but several of the warning signs spotted can represent poor management and sloppy hygiene standards.

Always check the Food Hygiene Rating
Remember that all food businesses that sell food direct to the final consumer are awarded a Food Hygiene Rating score of 0–5. Food businesses are encouraged to display their rating and are provided window stickers to do so. If you don't see a window sticker then you might want to ask yourself why. For more information on the scheme please visit our National Food Hygiene Rating Scheme – Information for Customers page.

What you should do if you think that the hygiene standards aren't up to scratch
- Complain to the manager or owner of the business
- Take your business elsewhere
- Report the business to us using the contact details below, or by using our online Food Hygiene, Licensing and Health and Safety Complaints Form (if the business is outside Rother then contact the local authority for the area). Please bear in mind before you contact us that we have a Food and Health and Safety Complaint Investigation Policy to help you understand what we can and can't deal with

Extract ③

More than 400 food outlets rated 'sub-standard' across North Wales

00:00, 30 APR 2012 | **UPDATED** 18:38, 27 MAR 2013 | **BY** WALESONLINE

THE food hygiene rating scheme was launched last year by the Food Standards Agency.

THE food hygiene rating scheme was launched last year by the Food Standards Agency. It rates the hygiene standards at every establishment which serves food on a scale from zero to five.

Any outlet rated one or zero is "sub-standard" and in need of major or urgent improvement.

As of Friday, April 27, there were around 300 places, from schools through to takeaways, which score a rating of one or zero – with 17 sites registering a zero rating.

The scheme is run by local authorities in partnership with the FSA. Local food safety officers carry out an inspection, and award an FSA food hygiene rating. As well as cleanliness the rating also looks at the condition of buildings – layout, lighting and ventilation – and how a business manages and records what it does to make sure food's safe.

Inspections are mandatory but businesses are under no legal obligation to display the ratings in store which is why the Welsh Government wants to change the law. However, the ratings of all businesses who have been inspected are available on the FSA website at www.food.gov.uk/ratings.

569 Shares

Activity ③

Now you are going to synthesize or combine what you have learned in a written answer. Using your table of information to help, answer the following exam-style question:

> **Explain what you have learned about the food hygiene rating scheme.**

Support

Be aware that when you synthesize or combine information, you are making clear what you have found out from the information you have read. There is no need to compare the details or to state where you got the information from. For example, you may state that the Food Hygiene Rating scheme operates in partnership with local authorities, but there is no need to say that you found out from two different sources that this is the case.

8 Comparing texts

Learning objectives

- To understand the term 'comparison'
- To explore how to compare information presented in texts

Key terms

Compare: to note the similarity or difference between two or more things

Comparison: a consideration of the similarities or differences between two or more things

In at least one of your English exams you will be asked to **compare** at least two of the texts you have read about. You will have already read and answered questions on them by this point. You may be asked to compare texts for a number of reasons. For example, you may be required to compare the viewpoints of two different writers or be asked to examine the effects of language within the texts. Be prepared to look at what information the writers put forward and the ways in which they do so.

Activity 1

In pairs discuss the types of words you might use when comparing one thing to another. Make a list of any vocabulary that you can think of. For example, *similarly, despite, conversely…*

Activity 2

The following two extracts both provide reviews of a restaurant called 'ffresh' in Cardiff. You are going to answer a question which asks you to compare the writers' views of this restaurant. Draw a table on your page like the one below and use it to make a note of the key evidence you will use. It may help you to organize your answer if you separate the views into positive and negative ones.

	Review 1		Review 2	
	View of restaurant	**Reason for view**	**View of restaurant**	**Reason for view**
Positives				
Negatives				

Activity 3

Using a highlighter pen, highlight any views that the writers share which are similar. In a different colour highlight any areas where they differ.

Activity 4

Use your notes to help you write an answer to the following exam-style question:

> **Both of these texts review the restaurant ffresh.**
> **Compare the following:**
> - **the writers' views of the restaurant**
> - **the reasons the writers give for their views.**

Review ①

◄ ▶ ↻ ⊠ +   🔍▾

Tuesday, 17 July 2012

'Get fresh!' – ffresh restaurant review, Cardiff

Another weekend, another pre-theatre dinner (it's a tough old life!) but this time the destination was ffresh, the in house restaurant underneath the rather wonderful Wales Millennium Centre. ffresh has been building a good reputation in Cardiff over the last couple of years [...]

We have been before as à la carte customers so we were looking forward to a good dinner.

When we arrived the Centre was buzzing and the bars were all full so we headed straight in to be seated. We were offered our choice of table and provided with the set menus at £18.50 for 2 courses or £22.50 for 3.

To start I ordered the Perl Las soufflé, port and fig jam and rocket salad. The twice baked soufflé was pretty good, but then I am a sucker for a soufflé. The texture was light and fluffy but the flavour was a little muted and I would have liked a stronger hit of blue cheese. I question the presentation of the brown smear of jam and the rocket salad was very tired and limp and a bit brown round the edges. [...]

For the main I had the 'Sirloin of Welsh beef, cottage pie, green beans and turnips'. The sirloin, like the salad, was a bit listless and dry, as if it had been sitting around under a heat lamp for just that bit too long. The cottage pie was decent enough, but nothing special and was frustratingly difficult to eat out of a deep narrow ramekin dish! [...]

As it was a set menu we decided to go for a dessert but I just didn't fancy any of the 3 options, none of them were screaming decadent to me so I went for the 'Selection of True Taste cheeses'. This was placed in front of me without ceremony and I had to call the waiter back to talk me through what was on it! The plate was made up of Perl Las, Perl Wen, Caerphilly and Y Fenni, some crumbly oat biscuits and a blob of chutney with grapes. All good quality cheese, the Caerphilly in particular was a winner, so no complaints from me. [...]

Overall we were happy with our meal but we have definitely had much better from ffresh when we have gone as à la carte customers and on a night when there wasn't a show on. My tiny gripe is that none of what we had was cooked 'ffresh' to order and as a result there were elements that felt a bit 'canteen-y' and this is a crying shame because this restaurant knows what it is doing. [...]

About...
A Cardiff food blog, about cooking and eating out in South Wales.

Review ②

◄ ▶ ↻ ⊠ +   🔍▾

Restaurant: ffresh, Wales Millennium Centre, Cardiff Bay

One of the great heroes of modern British cooking is behind the menu at one of Wales's foremost public spaces

John Lanchester

Friday 24 February 2012

[...] ffresh is round the back of the shiny-scaled Millennium Centre, known locally as the Armadillo. The restaurant has a view towards the bay and, on a bright, cold, winter day, is a lovely place to be [...]

The chef is Kurt Fleming, aided by one of the great heroes of modern British cooking, Shaun Hill, consulting on the menu. [...]

Translated through the necessary constraints of the location – that is, doing a lot of pre-theatre covers pretty fast – Hill's presence is felt in a menu that has an emphasis on the local and seasonal. You feel the need for speed in the starters, which are the least interesting part of the meal. Halloumi had that weird, super-rubbery texture it sometimes has, and its pepper and aubergine dressing was over-tweaked with capers. Confit of duck leg arrived as three room-temperature discs of uncharismatic, dry terrine with a smear of apple purée on the side. The salad with it, however, was a brilliant assembly of pea shoots, cubes of apple and black pudding. It had an extraordinary earthiness. I don't mean that metaphorically – it did genuinely taste of earth, as well as of greenery: a remarkable couple of mouthfuls.

With mains, the meal lifted off. Anthony Bourdain once said that it's impossible to avoid the word 'unctuous' when discussing pork belly. I surrender: the belly was unctuous, all fat rendered and the meat dense but soft. The accompanying cabbage was spiked with something, maybe allspice, that gave it a subtle, elusive sweet note to complement the pork. Fillet of bream, cooked with perfect technique, came on a bed of herb and anchovy risotto made with one of those softer, non-arborio rices, with a dollop of salsa verde adding a note of freshness and acidity to a beautifully balanced and flavourful plate.

Bread-and-butter pudding featured Brecon gin marmalade and came with a shot glass of lemon cream on the side, and the overall effect was masterly, sweet but sharp. [...]

Lunch was £15.50 for two courses – cracking value.

9 Editing tasks

Learning objectives

- To understand the term 'editing'
- To engage with some editing activities

Key terms

Editing: to choose material and arrange it to form a coherent whole

Verbal reasoning skills: skills which help you understand and comprehend information, like reason and deduction

In your Unit 2 English exam you will be asked to complete some **editing** tasks. These will be multiple choice questions and you will have to use **verbal reasoning skills** to work out which of the answers given is the correct one. This type of question may present itself in different ways – you may be asked to look at specific word choices, or figure out the combined effect of multiple words in a sentence, or you may be asked to examine a series of sentences and answer questions on their structure.

The following exam-style questions test your skills when looking at word-level choices. Look at the example below carefully.

Read the paragraph below and then answer the questions that follow:

Jonathan had a (1)_____ for chocolate. He would try to resist it but this rarely (2)_____ him from eating it.

(a) Circle the word below that best fits gap (1):

    A) weakness   B) respect   C) desire   D) basket

(b) Circle the word that best fits gap (2):

    A) defeated   B) affected   C) stopped   D) helped

Make sure that you read both sentences carefully before answering the question. If you look at gap (1) all of the words would make some sense if used in the gap. Knowing what follows in the second sentence makes it easier to discount some of them. The correct answer is A) weakness. For gap (2) the answer is C) stopped. The best way of making sure you have the right answer in these types of question is to ensure that the words you have placed in (1) and (2) make sense when you read both sentences together.

Activity 1

Try to answer the following:

1. **The dogs were (1)_____ with excitement. Their barks filled the air and they pulled and (2)_____ on their leads.**

   (a) Circle the word that best fits gap (1):

   A) happy   B) placid   C) frenzied   D) tired

   (b) Circle the word that best fits gap (2):

   A) strained   B) pushed   C) bit   D) snored

2. **Everything went (1)_____ for a moment and then came back into focus. He must have hit his head harder than he (2)_____ .**

   (a) Circle the word that best fits gap (1):

   A) light   B) away   C) black   D) home

   (b) Circle the word that best fits gap (2):

   A) managed   B) realized   C) fell   D) knows

The following exam-style questions test your skills when looking at sentence-level choices. Look at the example below carefully.

Read the paragraph below and then answer the questions that follow:

Circle the pair of words that best fit the meaning of the sentence below:

I was _____ to see my best friend again; this _____ was something I had long looked forward to.

(A) thrilled…place

(B) horrified…party

(C) delighted…reunion

(D) ashamed…meeting

(E) overwhelmed…journey

The correct answer is (C). The first gap must be a positive emotion because the second part of the sentence makes it clear that s/he was looking 'forward' to it. The use of the word 'again' in the first part of the sentence makes the word 'reunion' the most likely candidate for the second gap.

Activity 2

Try to answer the following:

1. **Sally was excited by the prospect of _____ her exams, just one more to _____ and they would all be over.**

   (A) taking…revise

   (B) finishing…recall

   (C) completing…go

   (D) marking…sign

2. **The Smith family set off for their _____ holiday; unfortunately they did not get very far before they _____ their missing passports.**

   (A) summer…picked up

   (B) annual…remembered

   (C) short…highlighted

   (D) life-changing…found

   (E) camping…knew

The exam-style questions on the next page test your skills when looking at text-level choices. Look carefully at the example that follows.

Read the paragraph below and then answer the questions that follow:

1. She had purchased all of the items on her list and was now ready to make her little boy's birthday cake.
2. She grabbed the scales and began to weigh.
3. Sugar and butter would be first into the mixer.
4. Wendy returned from the shop and unpacked the contents of her bag.
5. Putting the icing sugar and filling ingredients to one side, she laid out the things she would need initially.

(a) Which sentence should come second in the text?

(b) Which sentence should come third in the text?

The correct answers are that sentence 1 should come second, and sentence 5 should come third. Here is the correct order of the sentences:

Wendy returned from the shop and unpacked the contents of her bag. She had purchased all of the items on her list and was now ready to make her little boy's birthday cake. Putting the icing sugar and filling ingredients to one side, she laid out the things she would need initially. Sugar and butter would be first into the mixer. She grabbed the scales and began to weigh.

> **Tip** Sometimes you will be asked to consider an extract at word, sentence or text level. This means looking at it in different levels of detail:
> - Word level – thinking about an individual word in a text
> - Sentence level – thinking about an individual sentence in a text
> - Text level – thinking about the text as a whole piece.

Activity 3

1. Look at the correct order of the sample text above and discuss with a partner why the sentences follow in the order they do. Make a note of your findings.

2. Now try to answer the following text-level question:

Read the paragraph below and then answer the questions that follow:

1. She was a little concerned because they didn't even know whether she had passed.
2. Her mum added that the celebration was for how hard she had worked and the fact that she had done her best – the results would not make a difference to that.
3. Eleanor and her family were going out for a meal to celebrate how hard she had worked for her exams.
4. Speaking to them, she confessed that some of her friends were only getting treats and trips out once they had got their results.
5. Her dad only laughed at this and told her there would not be a reward come results day.

(a) Which sentence should come fourth in the text?

(b) Which sentence should come fifth in the text?

10 Formal letters

Learning objectives

- To understand how to set out a formal letter
- To explore audience and purpose

You would write a formal letter to a person or company that you do not know personally. If you do know them it may be in a professional capacity so you would also respond to them in a formal way. Letters of this type generally take quite a serious approach and are formal in their use of language and tone. You may wish to write this type of letter to persuade somebody to do something (or perhaps not do something), you may wish to share information or state your views on a particular subject, or you may wish to make a complaint and perhaps require an action to be taken.

The layout of a formal letter is fixed and you must follow certain conventions. Look at the guidance below and make sure you understand how to set out a formal letter.

Address of sender
(only the address is needed – don't include your name or phone number)

Date

Name of recipient (if known)
Job title of recipient (if known)
Address of recipient

Salutation
Dear Sir/Madam if identity not known or
Dear Mr… or Ms/Miss/Mrs… if name known

Introductory paragraph with clear statement to indicate reasons for writing
E.g. I am writing to…
Recently it has come to my attention…

A series of paragraphs with detailed information that develop your ideas in relation to the task

Concluding paragraph – include information on any results/actions that you would like to see taken as a result of your letter. Thanking the recipient may also be appropriate.

Signing off
Yours faithfully if identity not known (if you've used 'Dear Sir/Madam')
Yours sincerely if identity known

Activity 1

The layout of a formal letter is something which must be learned. There is a right way to do it and you need to ensure that you remember this information.

Design a colourful revision sheet containing this information that you will be able to refer back to during your GCSE English course.

Activity 2

Read the following exam-style question:

> **A café in your local area is advertising for part-time employees. Write a letter to apply for the position.**

Look again at the question and do the following:

1. Underline/highlight the word or phrase which makes it clear who your audience is (who you are writing to).

2. Underline/highlight the word or phrase which makes it clear what your purpose is (the reason for writing the letter).

Activity 3

Planning is essential for this kind of activity in order to make sure your ideas are presented as clearly as possible. Think about what kind of information your letter will need to contain and how you will demonstrate that you are focused on the purpose.

Using bullet points, a table or a spider diagram, plan out in detail what will be contained in the main part of your letter. For example:

What will they want from an employee?	What have I done to show those skills?
someone local	I live just outside the town centre...
someone...	

Activity 4

Using your plan and your revision sheet about how to present a formal letter, write a response to this question. You should aim to write between 350 and 500 words.

Progress check

Once you have proofread your work, swap with a partner to give each other feedback. Use the following prompts to target your comments:

1. How well have they adopted the conventions of formal letter writing?

2. Is their awareness of audience and purpose clear throughout?

3. Do they provide enough detail on themselves, or are there areas where this could be extended?

4. Are there any spelling, punctuation or grammatical errors in their work?

5. Could anything they write be expressed more clearly?

Assessment

Reading and understanding

Learning objectives

- To practise explaining information selected for an answer
- To begin to consider how writers use language to influence readers

Introduction

During this chapter you have learned and practised a number of techniques which will help you investigate and explore a text. The following extract and questions will help you to put some of these into practice.

Read the following extract about school dinners.

The School Dinner Scandal – Reporter Feature By: Tazeen Ahmad

Related Dispatches: The School Dinner Scandal

My nightly ritual for months has involved packing baby tomatoes and cucumber slices into one tub, throwing in a piece of fruit and the healthiest sandwich I can muster up into another, popping it all into a lunch box and placing it in the fridge overnight.

It's far from ideal but as a working mum I struggle to make a packed lunch in the morning. Why do I do it? My son won't eat school dinners.

Talking to other parents in the schoolyard, it's hard to know if we simply have fussy children or if the problem lies in the meals served in the canteen. He starts a new school this term so we've signed him up to the promise of new healthy, tasty school dinners; my fingers are very firmly crossed.

It was back in 2005 that Jamie Oliver first placed school meals under the microscope. His campaign led to a real change. Millions were pumped into improving school canteens and tough minimum standards on food and nutrition were enforced. Since then, Turkey Twizzlers, ketchup counting as a vegetable, and chips with everything was supposed to have been consigned to history.

But Dispatches has found that in the face of free markets in education and the profit margins of the big fast food chains, strategies to prevent childhood obesity have gone on to the back-burner. Seven years after his school food revolution, Jamie Oliver is disappointed that take-up is so low.

'The kids don't like the food,' he told me. 'It doesn't matter what the food is; organic, fresh or mass-produced rubbish, if it don't taste good, the kids won't eat it.'

He's also very concerned about the food sold in academies, now attended by around half of all school children in England. Under the coalition government's reforms the Education Secretary, Michael Gove, is keen to do away with red tape and council interference in schools. Academies have been given the freedom to run their own budgets and so they no longer have to abide by strict guidelines on food and nutrition.

The schools that do serve healthy meals face other challenges. Hundreds of schools allow pupils out at lunchtime and often they emerge to see fast food chains serving greasy chicken and pizza just yards outside the school gates.

Activity 1

Answer the following questions. Try to make sure your answers are clear, and detailed where they need to be. Make sure you use evidence from the text to support what you say.

1. Reading it in context, what do you think the word 'ritual' means in the first sentence?

2. Can you explain why this reporter's nightly ritual takes place?

3. Explain why the reporter says her 'fingers are very firmly crossed' at the end of the third paragraph.

4. What does the phrase 'placed school meals under the microscope' suggest?

5. Write down two positive things that came out of Jamie Oliver's initial campaign in 2005.

6. Explain the phrase 'consigned to history'.

7. What phrase does the article use to suggest that the prevention of childhood obesity is no longer of high priority?

8. How does this article emphasize Jamie Oliver's disappointment with the state of school food?

9. Explain why there is particular concern about the food sold in some academies?

10. Explain how the writer uses vocabulary and persuasive techniques to convey her negative feelings about the challenges faced by schools that do serve healthy meals.

Assessment

Planning to write

Learning objectives

- To plan and write an expository report
- To proofread and improve work

Introduction

In this writing assessment you will plan and write a formal report. Think carefully about the skills you developed earlier in this chapter and how you will incorporate them into your writing.

Activity 1

Read the following brief carefully:

Your school governors are determined to target the eating habits of children in your school. You are a member of the school council and you have been asked to write a report which explains the view of the students with regard to school dinners. You may wish to write about the meals, the condition of the school cafeteria and other aspects which influence the eating choices made by students. There may be positive information about what the school currently does that is a success and/or recommendations of the ways in which things could improve.

1. Write a detailed plan of what you will include in this report.

2. Share your plan with a partner. Discuss and note down any improvements that could be made to each of the plans. Also take the opportunity to check each other's work for any errors.

Support

Points to think about before beginning this task:

- Who is your audience?
- Why are you writing this report?
- What will the tone of the report be?
- What will the layout look like?

You may find it helpful to revise the structure of expository writing featured on page 77.

Activity 2

1. Look carefully at your plan. Write out in full one of your main argument/discussion points. This should be presented as one or two detailed paragraphs.

2. Now spend five minutes reading through what you have written to make sure it makes sense. Correct any mistakes and rewrite any areas where expression could be clearer.

3. Swap your work with a partner and ask them to check for errors and suggest any ways in which it could be improved.

Activity 3

Now write the remainder of the report. Insert the section you have already written and improved in the relevant place.

3 PEOPLE

In this chapter you will further develop a range of reading, writing and oracy (speaking and listening) skills. You will encounter a range of reading activities in which you can develop your ability to **synthesize**, analyse, reflect and evaluate. You will practise a range of writing skills including producing a review and some narrative writing. To improve your speaking and listening, you will develop both presentation and conversation skills.

The focus of this chapter is 'People'. The extracts you read will focus on different types of people – from both the past and the present. While you are reading and analysing the extracts, try to think about the appearance, behaviour and actions of the people within them and consider how you feel about them as a reader.

'The key to good decision-making is evaluating the available information…'
Emily Oster

'You never really understand a person until you consider things from his point of view – until you climb into his skin and walk around in it.'
Harper Lee, To Kill a Mockingbird

'True genius resides in the capacity for evaluation of uncertain, hazardous, and conflicting information.'
Winston Churchill

This chapter focuses on a wide range of text types – both **continuous** and **non-continuous**. Throughout this chapter you will focus on a range of the text types you have already covered in previous chapters. People feature heavily in almost every type of written text. From some of the earliest religious texts to newspapers, magazines, journals and contemporary books almost every text will include or be influenced by people.

Throughout the chapter you should consider how people are presented differently in each form of writing. Skilled writers will create believable characters who we can visualize, identify with, admire or even despise. The characters in fictional writing are made up by the writer but people in non-fiction are real. Real people can be presented in a certain light by the writer and the job of the reader is to recognize any bias or prejudice in the ways they are presented. Sometimes a reader will need to take information from more than one source to create their own interpretations and understanding of a person.

Key terms

Synthesize: to form something by bringing together information from different sources

Continuous text: text written in sentences and paragraphs

Non-continuous text: text which presents information in other ways, for example charts, tables, diagrams and graphs

Exam link

Exam relevance

In the exams you will be asked to read from a range of different texts and this chapter will give you the opportunity to develop some of the reading skills which will help you access this variety of material. You will also be given the chance to develop the presentation skills that are required for Unit 1.

In this chapter you will:

- read, analyse and evaluate a range of different texts
- synthesize information from a range of texts
- develop skills for the writing section of the exams
- consider how to present information in speaking and listening activities.

Exploring people

Learning objectives

- To explore the overall theme of people
- To reflect on your own experiences of people

Key terms

Evaluate: to form an idea of the state or value of something

Impression: effect produced on the mind, ideas

Introduction

The theme of this chapter is 'People'. Most of us will encounter hundreds of people each day, though we will only interact or communicate with a small number of them. Some people can be hugely influential in our lives, persuading us to dress or act in a certain way. Some people will become lifelong friends, while others may only feature in our lives for a short period of time. Throughout this chapter you will be reflecting on, analysing and **evaluating** people and their actions. By reflecting on the people you meet every day, you will broaden your understanding of texts without even thinking about it.

If you checked the dictionary for a definition of 'people', it would tell you they are:

1. human beings in general
2. men, women and children belonging to a place or forming a group or social class.

This certainly gives us a starting point, but it doesn't tell us much about the complexities of people, their amazing and terrible capabilities or the emotional reactions they can evoke in others. These are some of the things that writers explore in their work.

Activity 1

1. Make a list of the first ten people who come into your mind.
2. Think about each of these people – write down any words or phrases (both positive and negative) that you would use to describe each one.
3. Choose three of the people on your list. Discuss with a partner what you think or feel about each of them.

Activity 2

Look at the three images on the right. Have you seen any of these people before? Can you describe what each of them looks like? Write down any words or phrases you would use to describe the people pictured in them.

Image A

Image B

Image C

The language or words you chose to describe each person in the pictures will have been based on your first (or visual) **impression** of that person. When you approach a new text you may have an initial impression of the person or events described in that text. Once you have read the information you will have a closer understanding of the person or events and will have added to, or changed, your first impressions. When you are writing about a text for your exam, it is important that you record a range of ideas in your answer and support them with evidence from the text.

Activity 3

Think about any recent TV programmes, films or news reports you have watched or any books you have read. All of these probably featured people in various situations and scenarios. What was the first thing you noticed about the main person or character? Can you remember what they were wearing? What did they look like? How did they behave?

Design and complete a table like the one below to show your recent experiences of people, recording specifically your first impressions of each person. Think carefully about the words and phrases you choose to describe the people.

Source	Person encountered
BBC News	Female news presenter. Smartly dressed, eloquent, tried to give a balanced view of the events (does not give an opinion). Professional but relaxed.

People from the past

1 What does an evaluation involve?

Learning objectives

- To understand the meaning of the term 'evaluation'
- To consider why we evaluate

Introduction

This unit focuses on one of literature's most famous detectives. Sir Arthur Conan Doyle's fascinating stories about the world-famous detective Sherlock Holmes were written between 1891 and 1927, and remain hugely popular. Books, films and TV programmes are constantly being made about this super sleuth and his assistant Dr Watson. In this unit you will reflect on the information you read and develop your evaluation skills using a wide range of texts, all focusing on Sherlock Holmes.

Essentially, an evaluation is a judgement of something or someone. If you are asked to evaluate something, you are being asked to engage with a text or topic and think carefully about what is happening and how that might make you feel.

Activity 1

The first Sherlock Holmes short stories were published as a series in a magazine called *The Strand*.

1. Spend ten seconds looking at the original *Strand* illustration of Sherlock Holmes and Dr Watson on this page. Write down your first impressions of Sherlock Holmes (the character on the right) based on this image.

2. Now look more closely at the picture and answer the following questions.

   a) How is he sitting? What does his posture suggest?

   b) What is he doing with his hands? Why is he doing this?

   c) Describe his face. Why does he look so intense/direct?

   d) Write down your impression of his clothing. Why is he dressed differently from Dr Watson?

Activity 2

In recent years many different actors have played Sherlock Holmes. The pictures below show three of them.

Image A

Image B

Image C

NEW HOLMES. NEW WATSON. NEW YORK.

ROBERT DOWNEY JR.
SHERLOCK HOLMES
A GAME OF SHADOWS
DECEMBER 2011

JONNY LEE MILLER
ELEMENTARY
LUCY LIU

PREMIERES THURSDAY SEPT 27 10PM ONLYCBS©2HD

1. Compared to the original illustration of Sherlock Holmes on page 110, which image do you prefer, and why?

2. Choose one of the pictures. Write down as many adjectives and descriptive phrases that you can think of to describe the actor.

Throughout Activities 1 and 2 you have been asked to give your impressions and feelings about the images and you have been using a range of evaluation skills without even thinking, such as considering:

- what you like and dislike
- how the images compare to others
- your overall impressions.

Activity 3

Support

We use evaluation skills most of the time but rarely write down what we are thinking. Complete the following activity to help you evaluate a lesson at school.

Think about a really good lesson you have enjoyed at school. What made the lesson enjoyable? What did you learn? How was the lesson different from other lessons? What could you add to the lesson to make it even better?

Exam link

Straightforward evaluations will:
- give personal opinions
- show some understanding of the text
- give straightforward supporting evidence.

Confident evaluations will:
- give an overview of the text as a whole
- see patterns within the text
- probe and explore the text in detail
- include convincing and persuasive supporting evidence.

2 Personal reflection

Learning objectives

- To explore your reactions to a piece of text
- To evaluate your reactions to a character within a text

Tip If you are asked to evaluate your thoughts and feelings, you can use the first person to help you frame your answer (*I think…*, *I feel…*). If you are asked to consider the character or writer's thoughts and feelings, you can use the third person to help you frame your answer (*He thinks…*, *She feels…*).

When evaluating a text you may be asked to give a personal response. You should track through a text and consider your thoughts and feelings at various points to enable you to give a balanced personal evaluation. You might be asked to consider how a character is thinking or feeling in an extract – you need to track through the extract, collecting evidence and considering what the character might be feeling at specific points.

Read the following extract from a Sherlock Holmes short story

Extract from 'A Scandal in Bohemia' by Sir Arthur Conan Doyle

His rooms were brilliantly lit, and, even as I looked up, I saw his tall, spare figure pass twice in a dark silhouette[1] against the blind. He was pacing the room swiftly, eagerly, with his head sunk upon his chest and his hands clasped behind him. To me, who knew his every mood and habit, his attitude and manner told their own story. He was at work again. He had risen out of his drug-created dreams and was hot upon the scent of some new problem. I rang the bell and was shown up to the chamber which had formerly been in part my own.

His manner was not effusive[2]. It seldom[3] was; but he was glad, I think, to see me. With hardly a word spoken, but with a kindly eye, he waved me to an armchair, threw across his case of cigars, and indicated a spirit case and a gasogene[4] in the corner. Then he stood before the fire and looked me over in his singular introspective[5] fashion.

'Wedlock suits you,' he remarked. 'I think, Watson, that you have put on seven and a half pounds since I saw you.'

'Seven!' I answered.

'Indeed, I should have thought a little more. Just a trifle more, I fancy, Watson. And in practice again[6], I observe. You did not tell me that you intended to go into harness[7].'

[1] silhouette – a dark shadow seen against a light background
[2] effusive – making a great show of affection or enthusiasm
[3] seldom – rarely, not often
[4] gasogene – a device for creating fizzy water
[5] introspective – concentrating on your own thoughts and feelings
[6] in practice again – Holmes means Dr Watson is working as a doctor again
[7] harness – routine, everyday work

Activity 1

1. In the extract, Dr Watson has decided to visit Sherlock Holmes. To help you develop your ability to produce an **overview**, write down, in not more than 30 words, a summary of what happens in the extract.

2. With a partner, discuss your initial reactions to Sherlock Holmes. What type of person is he?

Key term

Overview: a general summary, explanation or outline of a situation

Activity 2

This activity will help you to build up your own thoughts about what type of person Sherlock Holmes is. Follow the steps below:

1. Go through the passage and highlight any phrases that you think give information about Sherlock Holmes. The first two have been done for you.

2. Write down the phrases you have selected in a table like the one below.

Evidence	What does this suggest?
'He was pacing the room'	He seems preoccupied or restless.
'head sunk upon his chest'	He seems dejected, troubled or deep in thought.

Activity 3

Use the table you completed in Activity 2 to help you answer the following question:

What are your thoughts and feelings about Sherlock Holmes?

To answer a question like this, you need to work through the extract in order (tracking the text), picking out any words and phrases that give you clues about his character. Cover the whole extract and do not repeat any ideas. Constantly ask yourself what you think and feel about him.

Support

The first few sentences have been done for you. Complete the answer using your own ideas and evidence.

I think that Sherlock Holmes is a preoccupied or restless individual. 'He was pacing the room' suggests he could be trying to collect his thoughts or solve a problem. Sherlock Holmes' head is 'sunk upon his chest' and I feel that this suggests he is deep in thought or reflection.

Activity 4

Look at your answer and use three highlighter pens to indicate the following:

- evidence
- your explanation
- the words 'think' or 'feel'.

You should see a balance of these three bullet points in your answer to ensure your response is focused and clear. If it is not balanced, go back and adjust your writing.

3 Persuasive writing

Learning objectives

- To explore the features of a review
- To plan a review

Persuasive writing is often involved when producing a review. After watching a film or TV programme, reading a book or listening to a CD, you will have opinions about it. To capture these opinions, you can write a review. The purpose of a review is not only to write down our views and opinions in an evaluation, but also to share them with other people who may wish to read about them.

A review is an evaluation. Reviews can consider books, articles, films, cars, buildings, art, fashion, restaurants, performances and many other products or services. It is important that a review is a commentary, not just a summary. You may like or dislike the thing you are reviewing, but you should always:

- state your opinions clearly
- give some supporting paragraphs
- come to a conclusion.

Activity 1

Below are the main features of a review. Read them carefully and put them in the correct order.

A Give a short summary of the piece. This includes a description and an idea of the purpose.

B In addition to analysing, a review often suggests whether or not the reader will appreciate it.

C Write down the title or name of the thing you wish to review.

D Offer a critical assessment (your evaluation). This should include your reactions, whether or not the piece was effective or persuasive, and your personal opinions.

Activity 2

When producing professional reviews for newspapers, magazines or online forums, writers think carefully about the language they select. To maximize the impact of their review or evaluation, a writer will try to use a range of different persuasive techniques (you have already studied many of these in this book). Match each technique in the list below to its definition.

Humour

Puns

Assertive point of view

Compare or contrast

Direct appeal

A 'You' is often used to encourage the reader to watch or read it

B To be clear and direct in your opinions

C Comparisons with other films or books are used to make it sound better or worse

D Something amusing or comical

E Humorous use of words or a play on words

Activity 3

Read the film review below and answer the following questions.

1. The reviewer refers to him as 'Swashbuckling Sherlock'. What does this imply about the character?

2. Highlight any persuasive techniques you can find in the review. Why do you think the writer chose to use persuasive techniques?

3. Look at the comparison used for the two Sherlock characters (you may wish to use a dictionary to work out what these words mean): Conan Doyle – 'complex, cerebral sleuth' and Guy Ritchie – 'bare-knuckle fighter'.

   a) What is the effect of the comparison?

   b) What does it suggest about Ritchie's Holmes compared to Conan Doyle's original?

4. Can you find any other comparisons? What effect do they have?

5. The writer tells us that the Holmes in the film is 'more indebted to comic strips'. What does this mean?

6. What does the writer mean when they tell us that the adventure is 'enjoyably silly'?

7. What does the writer mean by the comment 'The story is of little importance'?

LATESTRELEASES

Swashbuckling Sherlock: Robert Downey Jr returns as a gun-toting, fist-fighting Sherlock Holmes and he's terrific fun

Sherlock Holmes: A Game of Shadows (12A)

Admirers of Sir Arthur Conan Doyle's complex, cerebral[1] sleuth[2] should stay away from Guy Ritchie's second film about a bare-knuckle fighter of the same name, played by Robert Downey Jr as a smart-alec spoiling for a fight.

The film's villain, Moriarty, and his climactic[3] fight with Holmes are all that remain of Conan Doyle's short story, 'The Final Problem'.

Downey's version of the detective is essentially Sherlock Hams, a swashbuckling eccentric[4], none-too-distantly related to Johnny Depp's Captain Jack Sparrow from the *Pirates Of The Caribbean* films.

But though he is more indebted[5] to comic strips than Conan Doyle, his new adventure is an enjoyably silly romp[6]. The story is of little importance...

[1] cerebral – intellectual or linked to the brain
[2] sleuth – detective
[3] climactic – forming an exciting resolution or climax
[4] eccentric – slightly strange or unconventional
[5] indebted – owing gratitude to someone
[6] romp – rough and lively play

Verdict: Action and fun

★★★☆☆

Look at the way the writer blends facts about the film with their views about the actors and the storyline. This is an effective technique to use when producing a review because readers of reviews like to read a balance of fact and opinion.

Activity 4

Follow these steps to plan your own review.

1. Write down the title of a story you have read or a film you have watched.

2. Briefly describe the main action. A flowchart might help you recall the order of events.

3. Start to evaluate the characters, storyline, special effects and ending (or anything that was important to you). Spider diagrams can be helpful when you are noting down detail about a lot of different elements.

4. Consider the audience. Who will enjoy it (or not)?

5. Note down your general conclusions.

Support

1. Look at step 3. Make a list of any words you would like to use to help you state your opinions about the book or film.

2. Write a paragraph that uses these words and gives an evaluation of what you have watched or read.

Stretch

Look at step 3. Think carefully about the characters, storyline, costumes, soundtrack and anything else notable about the book or film. Write two paragraphs, giving a clear evaluation of what you have watched or read.

Tip Remember: it is perfectly acceptable to write a review about something you absolutely detest. Make sure you give direct and honest opinions about it, but back these up with reasons. You must explain why a film is awful if that's what you believe.

4 Conclusions in narrative writing

Learning objectives

- To explore reactions to a text
- To evaluate the effect of a concluding passage
- To understand what is meant by narrative writing

When you reach the end of a book, you may choose to spend a few minutes thinking about what you have just read. If the ending of the **narrative** is particulary shocking, you may feel stunned for a moment or two while you take in and process what you have just read. Good readers should be able to reflect on what they have read and evaluate it. Sometimes you might be asked to read a section of a narration or the concluding paragraph, and evaluate how effective you found it.

Examples of texts in the text-type category of 'narration' include a novel, a short story, a play, a biography, a comic strip and a newspaper report of an event.

Activity 1

Think about the books you have read or the films you have watched; you will have experienced a range of different endings, some of which you might use as ideas for your own writing.

1. What is your favourite book or film? How does it end? With a partner, discuss the ending in detail and try to explain why you enjoyed it.

2. With a partner, look at the following list of possible endings. Write down a brief definition for each of them.

   a) Cliffhanger
   b) Resolution
   c) Circular or 'tie-back' ending
   d) Fairy-tale ending
   e) The sermon

Sir Arthur Conan Doyle invented a deadly enemy, Moriarty, to kill off Holmes. Doyle felt that the success and popularity of Holmes was distracting the world from his other achievements. In 'The Final Problem', Moriarty made his most significant appearance, falling with Sherlock Holmes to a watery grave at Switzerland's Reichenbach Falls. The extract below describes Dr Watson exploring the area of his friend's death.

Extract from 'The Final Problem' by Sir Arthur Conan Doyle

I stood for a minute or two to collect myself, for I was dazed with the horror of the thing. Then I began to think of Holmes's own methods and to try to practise them in reading this tragedy. It was, alas, only too easy to do. During our conversation we had not gone to the end of the path, and the Alpine-stock marked the place where we had stood. The blackish soil is kept forever soft by the incessant drift of spray, and a bird would leave its tread upon it. Two lines of footmarks were clearly marked along the farther end of the path, both leading away from me. There were none returning. A few yards from the end the soil was all ploughed up into a patch of mud, and the branches and ferns which fringed the chasm were torn and bedraggled. I lay upon my face and peered over with the spray spouting up all around me. It had darkened since I left, and now I could only see here and there the glistening of moisture upon the black walls, and far away down at the end of the shaft the gleam of the broken water. I shouted; but only the same half-human cry of the fall was borne back to my ears. [...]

An examination by experts leaves little doubt that a personal contest between the two men ended, as it could hardly fail to end in such a situation, in their reeling over, locked in each other's arms. Any attempt at recovering the bodies was absolutely hopeless, and there, deep down in that dreadful caldron of swirling water and seething foam, will lie for all time the most dangerous criminal and the foremost champion of the law of their generation.

Activity 2

Read this sample exam question:

> **What do you think and feel about these lines as an ending to the passage?**

You may be asked to evaluate the ending of an extract or a story in an exam. You need to go through the indicated section and think carefully about the following:

- What happens?
- Why does it happen?
- How do you feel about it?
- What does the writer do to manipulate your feelings?
- How successful is the ending? (If appropriate, reflect back on the rest of the story.)

With a partner, discuss the questions above and apply them to the extract from 'The Final Problem'. Write down two or three of your initial responses to each of these questions.

Support

Look at the highlighted sections in the extract. They are evidence that something dramatic has taken place in the story. Choose four of these from across the extract and write them down. Next to each piece of evidence, write down briefly:

- what you think has happened
- what the evidence adds to the ending and why (e.g. 'It adds tension because…').

Stretch

The highlighted sections in the extract are evidence that something dramatic has taken place. Write down each piece of evidence and then evaluate its effect, considering how the evidence contributes to the ending. For example:

'I was dazed with the horror of the thing': this word 'dazed' implies that Watson is truly shocked by what has happened and the 'horror' confirms that something dreadful has happened. Readers share Watson's fears as they realize that this could be the end of Sherlock Holmes.

Tip Refer back to the question to keep your answer focused.

5 Judging a character

Learning objectives

- To develop your skills of speculation
- To explore a character and their behaviour
- To develop oracy skills for Unit 1

Some texts focus almost solely on one character. If you are given a text like this you will need to carry out a detailed character evaluation. In addition to stating the obvious things about the character, you will need to probe the text so you can make some informed judgements about their actions and appearance.

Activity 1

Look at the picture of the actor below who is playing a teenage Sherlock Holmes. Use the questions beside the picture to help you make some speculations.

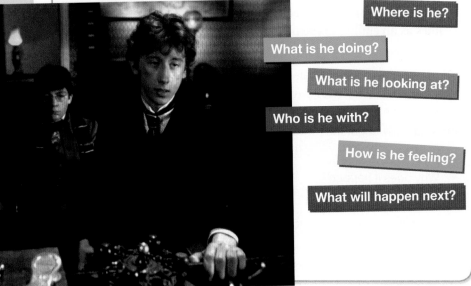

Where is he?

What is he doing?

What is he looking at?

Who is he with?

How is he feeling?

What will happen next?

Mycroft is Sherlock Holmes' older brother. In this extract, Mycroft has just taken the young Sherlock to their uncle's house for the summer.

Extract from 'Death Cloud' by Andy Lane

He turned towards Sherlock, and there was a look in his eyes that was part sympathy, part brotherly love and part warning. 'Take care, Sherlock,' he said. 'I will certainly be back to return you to school at the end of the holidays, and if I can I will visit in the meantime. Be good, and take the opportunity to explore the local area. I believe that Uncle Sherrinford has an exceptional library. Ask him if you can take advantage of the accumulated wisdom it contains. I will leave my contact details with Mrs Eglantine – if you need me, send me a telegram or write a letter.' He reached out and put a comforting hand on Sherlock's shoulder. 'These are good people,' he said, quietly enough that Mrs Eglantine couldn't hear him, 'but, like everyone in the Holmes family, they have their eccentricities. Be aware, and take care not to upset them. Write to me when you get a moment. And remember – this is not the rest of your life. This is just for a couple of months. Be brave.' He squeezed Sherlock's shoulder.

Sherlock felt a bubble of anger and frustration forcing its way up his throat and choked it back. He didn't want Mycroft to see him react, and he didn't want to start his time at Holmes Manor badly. Whatever he did over the next few minutes would set the tone for the rest of his stay.

He stuck out his hand. Mycroft moved his own hand off Sherlock's shoulder and took it, smiling warmly. 'Goodbye,' Sherlock said in as level a tone as he could manage. 'Give my love to Mother, and to Charlotte. And if you hear anything of Father, let me know.'

Activity 2

1. In the extract, Mycroft behaves carefully and deliberately as though he is warning Sherlock. Highlight any words or phrases that suggest Mycroft has concerns about leaving his younger brother.

2. Highlight any words or phrases that suggest how Sherlock is feeling about being left.

3. What does Mycroft mean when he says, 'they have their eccentricities'?

Activity 3

Work with a partner. Imagine you are being taken to visit a distant relative you have never met before. On the journey there, your older brother tells you that you will be staying for the whole summer.

1. Decide with your partner who is the older brother and who is younger. Spend five minutes on your own, jotting down some ideas. Think about:
   - how the conversation will start
   - the tone you will use and how this might vary
   - what you will say to one another
   - the body language/body position you will adopt when you are speaking
   - how you will react to each other
   - the types of questions you will ask
   - how the conversation will end.

   Thinking about these things will help you to act and answer questions in character.

2. Now have the conversation. Try not to refer to your notes too much as this will interrupt the flow of the conversation. Listen to what your partner says and try to respond spontaneously but in character, using your preparation to shape your answers and questions.

Progress check

You are going to carry out some peer assessment on Activity 3. With your partner, judge your performance based on the following criteria:

- If things went well, write down particular examples of what worked.
- If you found this a challenging activity, try to note down what happened; it will help you to understand how you could do it differently next time. For example, it can be difficult to respond 'on your feet' to what the other character said. Next time, you could try predicting what the other character might say and preparing some responses.

Exam link

You could be asked to produce an account of an occasion like this one as a descriptive task in your Unit 2 examination.

What did we do?	Very good – we did well at this.	OK – we were happy but need more practice.	We struggled with the activity.
managed to sustain the conversation			
listened closely to each other and responded thoughtfully			
challenged each other in a variety of ways			
each referred to things the other said throughout the conversation			

People today

6 Reflect and evaluate

Learning objectives

- To use reflection skills when considering what achievement is
- To develop evaluation skills
- To develop summary skills further

Key term

Achievement: something good or worthwhile that you have succeeded in doing

Introduction

In this unit you will look at people from across society and consider how their achievements are presented, and how they can be evaluated. You will continue to evaluate the impact of texts and the people in them while developing your skills in reading, writing, and speaking and listening.

What is **achievement**? We can't always remember our first taste of achievement – our first steps as babies or learning to feed ourselves. For some babies, simply leaving hospital after being born prematurely is an achievement. As we move through life, achievements can be small (making it to school on time) or large (academic success, developing sporting skills, or such things as overcoming emotional and physical barriers).

What do you think are achievements? Not everyone agrees on the same things. As you get older, your perception of what this is will also change. This will often depend on what an individual has done or achieved either for themselves or for the good of society.

Activity 1

1. What is achievement? Can any kind of success be an achievement?
2. The basketball player and coach John Wooden said, 'Never mistake activity for achievement'. Do you agree with him? Make a list of the kinds of thing you feel are achievements.
3. List three people who you feel have achieved something important.
4. What have these people done or achieved? Why do you admire them?

Think about what makes someone a hero or heroine. Often, achievements display an element of heroism.
You don't have to be a hero to achieve something, but can you be a hero without achievement?

Activity 2

In small groups, discuss this question:

Can you be a hero without achievement?

Listen carefully to the arguments each person in your group makes; you need to evaluate each one and decide whether you agree with it, and if not, express why you don't agree.

Activity 3

1. Look at Image A. What does this picture suggest about the firefighters?

2. Think about the way they are sitting. What does their posture suggest?

3. Look closely at their faces. What do you learn by the way they look?

4. Look at Image B. Why do you think the suit is empty?

5. Look at the writing at the top of the advert. Why does the writer use the phrase 'new suit'? What do you normally associate with a 'new suit'? Why is this effective?

Image B

Maybe It's Time To Add A New Suit To Your Wardrobe

Volunteer Firefighters Are Needed

Charlottetown Fire Department
89 Kent Sreet
www.city.charlotteotown.pe.ca
902-629-4083

Image A

Read the following article about Rosie Chisnell, a nurse. As you read, keep in mind the ideas about achievement you discussed in Activity 1.

'Other nurses clock on and off – she is a constant': Meet Rosie, the unsung hero of a nurse who fights for sick children's lives as if she was their mother

There was never any question over what Claire Rumble would call her daughter when she was born last month. It was always going to be Rosie, the name of the specialist nurse who looked after her big brother Louis during his three-and-a-half year battle with leukaemia. [...]

The family, who live in Hemel Hempstead, in Hertfordshire, first met Rosie in September 2009, after a terrifying five days when Louis became suddenly and desperately ill.

'One day he was fine, playing with his twin sister Grace, then suddenly he stopped eating, was pale, exhausted and crying through the night for no apparent reason,' recalls Claire. 'When angry purple bruises appeared all over his body we rushed him to hospital.'

Just 12 hours after a barrage of tests at Watford General Hospital doctors revealed the shocking diagnosis: the 19-month-old had leukaemia. 'You can't imagine what being told your son has cancer feels like,' says Claire. 'The world just stops.'

As the hospital's paediatric oncology nurse, Rosie, 56, was there at the diagnosis. 'For the next two hours Rosie sat with us explaining everything in great depth, fielding our questions and laying everything out clearly and honestly.' [...]

From day one the Rumble family had her mobile number. 'Children aren't ill nine to five, Monday to Friday,' explains Rosie. 'I would hate to think something might happen and a family couldn't get hold of me.'

Claire and James, a 37-year-old aircraft engineer, frequently had to call Rosie late at night when Louis developed croup – a fierce barking cough – because of his weak immune system. [...]

Once Louis accidentally pulled out his nasogastric tube – a tube inserted via the nose into the stomach to administer medication. Unfortunately, it was on a weekend when Rosie wasn't working, but she knew putting it back would be a traumatic experience for a child, so dropped everything and drove the 40 minutes from home to the hospital to do the procedure herself. [...]

The next day Rosie called to say not to take Louis to hospital as she was coming to their house with the equipment to teach Claire how to administer the intravenous antibiotics at home.

'I couldn't believe anyone could be so kind. She arrived with a great crate of equipment and stayed until almost midnight, showing me exactly how it all worked; the pump, the syringes, everything.

'Louis's face lights up when he sees her and when he was in hospital if he heard her heels click-clacking down the corridor he would sit up in bed. [...]

'For a parent, you can't underestimate the impact of having someone like Rosie around. I'd have spent days stewing over Louis's health, endlessly worrying, but Rosie being just a phone call away meant I was less anxious and felt more in control. She helped me and James to focus on the practicalities of his treatment and be better parents.'

So what drives this kind of dedication? 'It's the children,' Rosie explains. 'They're a model to us all. They just get on with it, the good and the bad. If I can improve their lives, or their families', even a bit, I'm happy.

'I know in this job I can make a difference. I've always loved children and got on with them easily and even as a little girl knew I wanted to be a nurse.' [...]

Rosie is adamant that she wouldn't be able to provide such high standards of care without the help of her colleagues. 'I couldn't be nearly so flexible without a strong team behind me.'

One member of that team is Vasanta Nanduri, a consultant paediatric oncologist who has worked with Rosie for the last 18 years. She says: 'She's my right hand, a great friend with far too much energy and someone I trust implicitly.

'But it's her knowledge and dedication to the children which is so impressive. She works out of hours, late into the night. She rarely takes a holiday, even though we try to make her. If she does, she writes 50-page handover notes. She's a real inspiration. Everyone on the ward looks up to her.'

Sentiments echoed by Claire. 'It will be a sad day when Rosie retires and I feel sorry for the families who won't get to meet her. We felt lucky every day that she was around and now we'll always be reminded of her kindness by baby Rosie.'

Activity 4

In this activity you are going to use your reading skills to write an evaluation of Rosie Chisnell. Follow the checklist to help you write an answer to the question:

Evaluate what you think Nurse Rosie Chisnell has achieved.

1. Read through the text, highlighting any words and phrases that show the following:

   a) what she has achieved for herself

   b) what she has achieved for other people

   c) how other people feel about her.

2. Look at the words and phrases. Think about these and explain why you think something has been achieved. You might like to annotate the text so you don't forget your ideas.

3. Write up your answer, one word/phrase at a time. Make sure you refer to the question so you are continually focused on what has been achieved. Try to keep each explanation focused, brief and clear.

Activity 5

Use the summary skills you have been developing in this book to produce a summary of what Rosie Chisnell has done to help Claire Rumble's family.

- Write your summary using bullet points.
- Aim to use no more than 10 bullet points in your answer.

Support

On pages 118–121 you have focused on firefighters and a nurse as people who have achieved. Can you think of any other groups of people whose achievements help to save the lives of others? Make a list of the qualities that these people need to help them with their work.

Stretch

You have been asked to help a design team to plan a poster encouraging people at school or college to take up a career as a doctor, nurse or carer. You will need to consider the following:

- how you could persuade young people to take up a career as a nurse, doctor or carer

- the qualities these people need to offer

- the type of picture/graphics you would use in the appeal

- the persuasive techniques you would use to appeal to your target audience.

Draw a rough plan of your poster. You do not need to draw any pictures – a description of the picture will suffice. Plan carefully the words you would include to persuade people to take an interest in your poster.

7 Presentation skills

Learning objectives

- To plan a presentation and consider how to deliver it
- To explore the verbal and non-verbal techniques used during a presentation

Oracy, or speaking and listening, makes up 20% of your final GCSE mark. You will have to complete one individual researched presentation as part of the oracy element of the assessment. The following activities and advice should help you to prepare for this section of your final assessment.

Giving a presentation to an audience, large or small, can be a terrifying experience. Presenters worry about many things including how people will respond to them, whether they will be heard, what questions will be asked, how they will manage to remember everything and so on. To ensure a presentation goes well, you need to think about two main things:

- What am I going to say?
- How can I present myself effectively?

Activity 1

Imagine you have been asked to give a presentation about the achievements of your school or college. Follow the steps below to help you plan what you will say.

What do you want to include? Before you start, it is a good idea to note down all the things you would like to talk about.

Prioritizing your information. Once you have decided on your main areas, you need to work out how you will sequence them. Think about which points are your key ideas, as you might like to place them at strategic points in your presentation.

What are your key messages? Some students like to highlight their key messages under each of their bullet points to prompt them when they are talking. Some students like to make a list of key words to use when they are talking.

Techniques to engage your audience. Once you have a rough plan for your speech you can go back through and give some consideration to the techniques you would like to include to engage your audience.

Final version. Now that you have your plan you need to produce a neater version. If your plan is very untidy you will struggle to use it effectively during your presentation.

Rehearsal. Now you need to rehearse your speech!

1. Complete a mind map or other planning tool with a partner to show the areas you would like to cover in your presentation.

2. Take the items from your plan and bullet point them in the order you would like to talk about them.

3. Under each bullet point add your key words and phrases. Try to avoid writing down complete sentences or you may end up just reading them from the sheet and losing fluency and effective non-verbal techniques.

4. Look at your rough plan to see where you can improve your language and add persuasive techniques. Rhetorical questions and repetition are particularly effective when delivering a speech (if used sparingly) but remind yourself of other persuasive techniques on pages 114–115.

5. Write up your plan either on cue cards or your tablet, paper or computer – whichever is best for you.

Here is the start of a student's plan for this activity. You can use it to help you get started.

1. What does achievement mean in my school? What have students achieved?

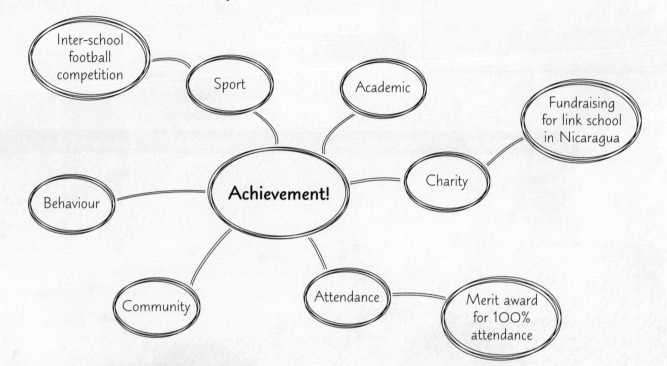

2. Which are most important?
   - Sport because we're a specialist school and students come here because of that
   - Academic
   - Charity

3. Most important points for achievement in each area:
   - Sport: specialist school; unbeaten record inter-school football; students come here because of sports department
   - Academic: good GCSE results; improved A-Level results; new science equipment to promote achievement
   - Charity: link to local community; sharing and caring; voluntary work; personal skills

   REMEMBER: make sure audience aware of my key messages. Use headings to make them stand out?

4. Which techniques will engage the audience?
   - Address audience directly, make them feel they want to come to our school
   - Use positive vocabulary
   - Build feeling of positivity from the start — with rhetorical Q 'Is there anything West Stanton Academy doesn't know about achievement?'

Tip It is a good idea to rehearse your presentation before presenting to an audience. Always speak out loud when rehearsing so you can practise when you will pause and which words you will emphasize.

Non-verbal features are all the non-talking things that accompany your presentation. They include the way you stand, the gestures you might make and the expressions on your face. Think about the presentations you have seen at school or interviews on the TV and what the speakers do to engage their audience.

Activity 2

1. Watch a TV or online news broadcast. Study the news reporter and take notes on what they do while they are talking. Record your findings in a table like the one below.

Facial expressions	Body movement	Hand movement	Props used

2. Think carefully about the news reporter. How did they emphasize a point using non-verbal features?

3. Did you find it easy to concentrate on what they were saying? Why?

4. How effective was the news reporter in engaging an audience?

Activity 3

Look at the transcript of an award speech below. In it, Declan Donnelly gives an acceptance speech for a surprise award marking his and Anthony McPartlin's 25 years of achievement in TV.

National Television Landmark Award 2013 Transcript

Declan Donnelly: This is kind of crazy and a bit bizarre but em, it's just the weirdest, weirdest thing ever.

There's so many people that we should thank for helping us in the past 25 years since we started when we were er eleven years old, um, when we got our first jobs, mine on *Byker Grove* and Ant's on *Why Don't You* as part of the Newcastle gang. There's hundreds of people that we've worked with and they've helped us and have taught us, er, everything we know and, we couldn't go into thanking every single person but every single person has put us on that journey and has put us here today. [...]

Erm, but it's just amazing. Thank you to, um, ITV, to James Grant, to everybody, um, that we've worked with from *Byker Grove* to our early days, erm, our first prime time job on the BBC, on *Friends Like These*. Thank you for that, erm, and for everybody we've ever worked with who has taught us, who has informed us, who contributed to who we are now, erm, but, but and everybody who featured there. But most importantly I think, you know, neither of us would be here if it wasn't for each other. So, ah.

Thank you so much, so, so much. Thank you everybody. Good night.

Award speeches are often unscripted. The speakers are often very emotional and have to give a speech in front of a large audience with no notes.

Activity 4

1. Look at the speech above. Do you think the speech is effective?
2. What do you notice about the speaker's use of language and grammar?
3. What would you change if you had to improve this speech? Use the steps in the plan on page 122 to make sure you consider every element.

8 Evaluating a newspaper article

When you evaluate a text that has been written about a person, it is important that you understand exactly why the article was written about them. The text below was written about Laura Trott before she became an Olympic champion. Laura was interviewed by *The Guardian* newspaper and, as the title of the article suggests, she was determined to win a gold medal.

Learning objective

- To evaluate a newspaper article and consider the effect it has on a reader

Laura Trott sick to the stomach in pursuit of 2012 glory

The Great Britain cyclist tells Donald McRae of the lengths she will go to in her bid for two gold medals

'I love the pain,' Laura Trott says, opening her eyes wide as she imagines the hurt that will accompany her pursuit of at least one gold medal at the Olympic velodrome this summer. 'Everyone goes on about the lactic burn and all that. They talk about the weird feeling you get in your mouth when the pain is bad – it tastes like blood – but I love that feeling. That's just me.'

Trott emits one of many infectious laughs, and then hammers home her point. 'Coping with that pain is the difference between winning and losing,' the teenage cyclist says as she prepares for a World Cup event in London later this month. 'You know it's going to [...] get you at some point in a race. But you can't exactly stop, can you? The important thing is to ride through the pain. I come out the other side and I'm going a heck of a lot better then.'

She is at her most interesting when detailing the physical trials she has survived in her short life. Born with a collapsed lung, which threatened her life, Trott then overcame asthma while continuing to struggle with an ailment that means she vomits after almost every race and serious training session. [...]

Trott [...] describes what happens to her on the track. 'They've given me some tablets to calm it down because I have such a high acid lining in my stomach. Whenever I tense, dead hard, it pushes all the acid up and makes me throw up. I've been throwing up since I was 10. As soon as I stop I can't control it for long. The worst was at the [2010] Commonwealth Games. It was on telly, wasn't it? Me being sick in a bucket.' She covers her face in mock embarrassment. 'But the tablets are working. I did a sprint the other day and didn't throw up afterwards for the first time in years.' [...]

The Olympics might see Trott emerge as one of the most distinctive faces in British sport – and it's easy to imagine the country going crazy about her with a couple of medals around her neck. 'I do think about how different life will be afterwards,' she says before a small smile breaks into another riotous laugh. 'But, right now, I'd better focus on winning the [...] thing!'

Activity 1

1. What is the purpose of this text?

2. Why do you think *The Guardian* chose to write an article about Laura Trott?

3. To be able to analyse and evaluate a text, you need to understand what it is about. Write down no more than five words to summarize each paragraph. For example:

   1. enjoys the pain of competition

4. List the problems Laura has faced in her life.

5. What do you think drives her to win?

6. Trott seems light-hearted and fun during the interview. Make a list of any words that suggest this.

Exam link

Remember to analyse each reading question very carefully in the exam before you begin your answer.

- Ask yourself what you will need to do in order to answer the question.
- How will you structure your answer and what will you include?
- Remember to consider the number of marks available in the time allocated when working out how long to spend on each answer.

Activity 2

Using the article for reference, answer the question:

What are your thoughts and feelings about Laura Trott and her achievements?

Support

Use the table below to help you to plan an answer to the question. Think carefully about the answers you gave in response to Activity 1 as these will help you to cover a wide range of different areas in your answer. Try to cover the whole text. Give yourself ten minutes to complete your plan.

What are your thoughts and feelings?	Evidence
She enjoys pushing her body to the limit...	'I love the pain'

Stretch

1. Use the skills you have developed throughout this book to answer the exam-style question above. Remember to support your answer with evidence from the text. You should spend no longer than 15 minutes writing up your answer.

2. When you have written your answer, spend 5 minutes checking it against the following assessment criteria. If you have missed anything, annotate your answer in a different colour:

   - I have taken evidence from across the text.

   - I have supported each piece of evidence with an explanation as to how it makes me feel.

   - I have covered a range of different aspects of Laura Trott's personality, background and achievements.

   - I have tried to vary the vocabulary I have used in my answer.

9 Commonly confused words

Learning objectives

- To check your use of homophones
- To produce a personalized list of spellings to revise

Tip Dialect can cause errors that come across in writing. Some students may use *are* instead of *our*, while others use *a* instead of *I*. Although these errors might seem very minor they will affect the mark you are awarded in your exam.

When you are producing a piece of writing it is important that you try to make your work as accurate and as clear as possible. Remember, half of your marks for the writing section of your exam will come from writing accurately: the vocabulary you choose, your use of grammar, and the accuaracy of your spelling and punctuation. Many GCSE students make careless errors with the selection and spelling of simple words, especially homophones. In this lesson, you will have the opportunity to check your knowledge of some of those commonly confused words and then correct them.

Activity 1

Below are some homophones that are most commonly confused. Go through the list and write a sentence with each one in. If you do not know the difference, look them up in a dictionary or ask your teacher.

- affect/effect
- their/there/they're
- where/were
- of/off
- to/too/two
- practise/practice

Activity 2

Look at the passage below. The writer has used many incorrect words. See if you can spot all the errors and correct them. SPAG

Jake and I had bin an item for months now. I was in every top set at school, he was struggling to get bye. I tried to help him as much as I could – staying in two revise and sharing my notes but it wasn't doing him any good.

One night while we where having a brake from are studies, he came up with a plan. 'Nobody collects in mobile devises in the exam and their are hardly any invigilators checking up on us,' he said. 'How about I use my phone to text you for advise?' Of coarse it was a huge risk but I wanted to help.

On the morning of the exam I felt sick. Mum tried to make me feel better. 'You have a flare for these things. You're dad and I are so proud.' I forced a smile. How could I except her compliment in this situation?

Halfway threw the exam I felt my pocket vibrate. I past my hand over my pocket but couldn't do it. Again and again I felt my pocket shake, it was having a dreadful affect on me. I was shaking and sweating and could bearly hold my pen. Five minutes to go. I couldn't bare it any longer. No one was watching. I slowly put my hand into my pocket. My fingers touched the cold metal screen but before I could take it out a hand clenched my shoulder. 'Can you please stand up Miss Jones?'

Activity 3

There are a number of common spelling errors that can be found in students' work. Look at the passage below and see how many spelling errors you can detect. Copy out the text, correcting all of the errors.

SPAG

Tip Over the coming months, make a list of the spelling errors that you make. You might like to display it somewhere where you will constantly see it to help you remember the correct spellings.

When using a computer you also need to take care, especially when using a spell-checker. If you are not careful you might select the wrong correction and completely change the meaning of what you write.

The que was enormous, like a huge snake it rapped itself around the building and dissappeared into the distance. There were allready alot of exited people standing with their family and freinds. It was quiet embarasing on this ocassion to be standing on my own. Choas broke out to my write where two women were having a viscious arguement about who would sucseed in the race to get to the shoe isle.

A couple at the back of the queue were stretching their muscles as though warming up for excercise. Standing seperately from his partner, the man clearly felt it nessessary to prepare for the exertions a head. His partner was having grate difficultie keeping her face strait as she copied his moves.

Suddenly the enviroment became more hostile. One woman began to remove her jewelry as she readied herself for the compitition. As I looked across at the other competetors, I sincerley began to wish I had stayed in bed. This was truely aweful. With a deep breathe, I turned and walked away.

People like you

10 Humour

Learning objectives

- To explore the different types of humour
- To plan a piece of amusing descriptive writing

Introduction

This final unit will give you the opportunity to think about how to communicate information in a lively manner. Think carefully about the tasks you are given when you are asked to write to a familiar audience and consider whether a humorous approach would be suitable. Remember to think about the role of humour in a text for effect.

You will now explore different types of humour. Humour can make us laugh out loud, but depending on the type of humour it can also make us slightly uncomfortable. It can make us reflect on our own behaviour or it can lift our spirits.

Activity 1

Make a list of the things that make you laugh. Are there any specific people who you find amusing? Do any specific situations amuse you?

Activity 2

There are many different types of humour. Can you match the definition to the type of humour?

Anecdote   Parody   Sarcasm

Irony   Farce

A A remark that seems to be praising someone or something but is really taunting or cutting – it can be used to hurt or offend, or for comic effect

B The use of words where the meaning is the opposite of their usual meaning or what is expected to happen

C A short entertaining story

D An imitation of something – particularly literature or a film – that is meant to make fun of it

E Something that is intended to be seen as ridiculous, particularly a comedy based on an unlikely situation

Writers use a range of techniques to make anecdotes about relatively mundane events and these often sound very comical. People often **exaggerate** to make the incident seem even more humorous.

> **Key term**
>
> **Exaggerate:** to make something seem larger, better or worse, or more important than it really is

Activity 3

Think about an event, book or story that has made you laugh.

- What happened in the moments leading up to the amusing incident?
- Who was there?
- What happened before the incident?
- What happened during the incident?
- What were people's reactions?

In the following extract, comic writer Stuart Maconie writes about a childhood trip to Blackpool. Look at the annotations to see how he gives some specific details.

The writer casually suggests he was in danger.

The writer uses unusual vocabulary to describe usual people.

This means bizarre and is blunt.

Again, a blunt description.

Seems an extreme treatment.

Extract from *Pies and Prejudice* by Stuart Maconie

Blackpool is one of my earliest memories. [...] Working-class Lancastrians go or at least went to Blackpool so often and so regularly – for day trips, holidays, stag dos – that it's impossible to date accurately when my first trip was. The mid-sixties I imagine. Probably in a romper suit and on reins, always being likely to stray under a passing tram to Cleveleys.

I remember my first proper holiday there in an abstract way, anyway. We were with my Auntie Mollie and Uncle Cliff and Cousin Steven. The boarding house was full of Scottish people. They were the first Scots I'd ever met and seemed tremendously exotic creatures to me, with their milky skins, freckles, outlandish accents, incendiary ginger hair and a massive capacity for sticky orange fizzy pop that tasted like metal. One of them was a fat boy of about twelve who got so sunburned that he spent the rest of the week in bandages and cotton wool. Sotto voce, people were sympathetic but they did say it was his own fault. What with his skin and everything.

The writer gives unusual extra details, e.g. clothing.

The writer uses proper nouns to give clear details.

This means flammable and is not a description we expect.

Funny description for a well-known drink – Irn Bru.

Activity 4

Think of a place that you know well. You are going to write a lively and humorous guide to the area, featuring yourself. To help you write your guide, use the spider diagram on the right.

Think about the language you could use and the specific details you could include to make your writing lively. Plan five or six topic sentences, one to help you write each paragraph.

Where are you writing about?

What are the main features of the place?

Are there any amusing aspects/people/incidents that have happened there?

Planning a humorous guide

How will you feature – as an observer or as part of something that happens?

What do you like/dislike about the place?

Assessment

Reading and understanding

Learning objectives

- To practise evaluative reading skills
- To practise wider reading skills
- To revise reading objectives

Introduction

During this chapter you have focused on the skills you need to be able to evaluate texts and characters. The extract below and the following questions will test your understanding of these skills and your ability to use them. Make sure you read the extract carefully and approach the text and your answers **chronologically**.

In this extract, Sara Maitland describes a period of heavy snow in County Durham.

Extract from *A Book of Silence* by Sara Maitland

Part of me became increasingly scared [...] What would happen if the weather did not improve? Was my family all right? But more of it was emotional – despite the fact that I was supposedly longing for quiet. I increasingly felt invaded. The silence was hollowing me out and leaving me empty and naked.

The cold intensified that sense of being exposed, and sometimes when the weather was particularly wild just getting the coal in from the coal shed was exhausting and even frightening. When the weather was calmer, however, I realised that snow produces a peculiar acoustic effect: it mutes nearby noises (presumably because the softer ground surface absorbs them) but causes distant sounds to carry further and with startling clarity. In addition the snow itself flattened everything visually. These effects disorientated me and made me increasingly nervy and jumpy. One day walking to my gate, the collar of my jacket blew up against the back of my head and I screamed aloud, viscerally[1] convinced I had been attacked from behind.

One afternoon I needed to break out and I took a walk up the undriveable road, despite the fact that there were flurries of 'snail' (a mixture of snow and hail) which, driven by the harsh wind, cut into my face. Then about half a mile from the house, I started to hear the most agonised wailing noises – the wailing, it seemed to me then, of the damned. I was completely terrified. I would be on this hill in this wind forever howling and desolate. I would never see another human being again. I would freeze in hell. It turned out that this strange and deeply disturbing noise was in fact no manifestation[2] of my inner torment, but caused by a strange and fascinating phenomenon. The unfenced roads in that part of the north-east have snow poles – tall posts marked in black and white foot-wide strips that show you both where the road is and how deep the snow is. Older snow poles are made of iron and have holes drilled in them for the wind to pass through. Essentially they were Aeolian harps[3] or organ pipes and they were responding to the wind with these extraordinary sounds. But I know I was lucky that I identified the source of the noise fairly quickly, because otherwise it would have driven me insane. I can only too easily understand how this sort of silence can drive anyone beyond panic and into true madness.

[1] viscerally – in a way that comes from deep inward feelings
[2] manifestation – an outward display
[3] Aeolian harp – a stringed instrument that makes sounds when the wind blows through it

Key term

Chronologically: in the order in which things occurred

Activity 1

1. Why is Sara scared in the first paragraph? **[3]**

2. What does the writer mean when she says, 'The silence was hollowing me out and leaving me empty and naked'? **[2]**

3. Look at paragraph 2. What are Sara's thoughts and feelings about the snow and the cold weather? You must refer to the text to support your answer. **[5]**

4. Explain why Sara was terrified in paragraph 3. You must refer to the text to support your answer. **[10]**

5. We realize that noise is a major concern for Sara. Look back across the whole text. What does Sara think and feel about the noises she hears in this extract? You must refer to the text to support your answer, for example: **[10]**

> Sara comments that 'The silence was hollowing me out and leaving me empty and naked,' which makes me think that she feels very uncomfortable about silence. The 'hollowing' suggests that the absence of noise makes her feel empty as though it is weakening her. On top of this, 'naked' sounds as though the silence is making her feel particularly vulnerable.

Tip When you are asked to refer to the text to support your answer, you are being advised to include evidence from the text (or quotations) to support each of the points that you make in your answer. Some students find it helpful to highlight sections of the text that they intend to use in their answer to ensure that their response remains chronological.

Try to vary the vocabulary you use in your explanations. For example, when exploring the evidence don't continually use the word 'terrified' to show that she is frightened. Instead you could use: *afraid*, *petrified*, *apprehensive*, *anxious* or *uneasy*. You can also be creative in your vocabulary when explaining an effect: *'this shows that...'*, *'this suggests...'*, *'from this we can infer...'*, *'her choice makes it obvious that...'*.

How you make your point is as important as the point itself, and demonstrating a variety of vocabulary shows you have a mastery of language, which is something the examiners are looking for.

Assessment

Proofreading

Learning objectives

- To develop proofreading skills
- To practise proofreading a range of documents

Tip
- Take your time. If you rush, you will miss errors.
- Read the passage or text one sentence at a time to see if it makes sense.
- Look for spelling errors or areas that do not make sense.

Exam link

When you are asked to proofread in the exam you must follow the instructions carefully. You will be asked to identify each error and then correct it. Make sure you clearly identify the error (underline, circle or highlight it) and then clearly correct it.

What is proofreading?

When you are asked to proofread a text you are being asked to read through the information very carefully to see if there are any errors. You need to check the text thoroughly to see if there are errors in the grammar, style, expressions or spellings. You will be tested on your proofreading skills in Unit 2 of the exam.

Activity 1

You will see many errors in day-to-day life. Try to see if you can spot and correct them. Look at images A–C and see if you can both identify and amend the errors.

Image A

Image B

Image C

Activity ②

Look at the extracts below. Identify and correct the errors in each one. In the exam you will usually be asked to identify five errors; some of the examples below may have more than five to find.

SPAG

Extract ①

Come in and enjoy the best sandwitch in Wales.

With a wide range of tasty snacks availible you wont be disappointed.

Todays specials

- Ham and cheese special
- Tosted burger and crunchy salad
- Classic bagette and french fries

Extract ②

Subject: Warning

Dear customer,

Please be aware that syber thieves are targeting our valued customers. If you recieve any emails requesting your personnel details then beware. Froudsters are targeting the public by asking them to log in to there personal accounts so they can verify their detales. Once you have logged in, you will usully be asked to give you're password. The tricksters then take a copy of your password so they can log in to your account at a later date and steal all of your money.

If you have any concerns please contact a member of our customer service team

Regards,

The Manager

Extract ③

We currently have space for two familes this weekend. The acomadation is perfect and comes highly reccommended in the AA's guide to good hotels. Fancy treating yourself to a spar? In our award winning beauty complex you can be pampered to your hearts content. The hotel does not cater for families and children must be a mimimam of 16 to enjoy are facilities. What are you waiting for. For a great day of relaxing and fun, start your prefect holiday this weekend.

Vacent – Special Offer

Exam link

When asked to proofread in the exam, spend a few minutes reading the text before you begin making corrections. The examiner will want you to be able to work in three different ways to proofread a text:

Text level – thinking about the text as a whole piece

Sentence level – thinking about an individual sentence in a text

Word level – thinking about an individual word in a text

Reading the whole text first will help you work out whether it makes sense as a whole piece of writing. Then check the text makes sense at a sentence level, before checking for errors in individual words.

Remember, if there are five marks available you should look for five errors.

Assessment

Writing

Learning objectives

- To plan and write a piece of persuasive writing
- To structure your writing and ideas purposefully

Introduction

In this assessment you will have the opportunity to plan and write a review. Think carefully about the skills you have developed throughout this chapter and make sure you incorporate them into your writing.

You read the following review in a movie blog:

HOME ABOUT CONTACT

… the film was absolutely atrocious. Having carefully read a number of reviews praising the director, the actors and the storyline, I can't believe I wasted my entire Friday evening watching such utter rubbish. This movie has been voted for a number of awards and I honestly believe this year's critics are either blind or are being blackmailed.

The acting was abysmal, indeed my 84-year-old grandmother could have performed some of the stunts with more enthusiasm…

Overall, this has to be the worst movie I have ever had the pain of watching. Thankfully I fell asleep before the end.

REVIEWS

Activity 1

Imagine that the review you have just read was written about your favourite film. Write a review of your favourite film.

Planning

You should spend five minutes planning your work. Think carefully about how you are going to evaluate the film – making your opinions clear for the reader. Think carefully about the structure of your review. Make sure you cover a wide range of different angles about the film.

You may find it helpful to revise the structure of a review on page 115.

Points to consider before you start:

- Who is your audience?
- What will your opening sentence be?
- Why not plan four or five topic sentences that will begin each paragraph in your writing?
- Will your review be serious or will you include some humour?
- Do you want to make a brief reference to the negative review you have just read?

Peer-assessment

Share your plan with a partner. Make notes on each other's plans if you can think of any ideas or points that could be included in their work.

Activity 2

Now spend 30 minutes writing your review.

Self-assessment

Now that you have completed your work, spend two or three minutes reading through it to make sure it makes sense.

Tips for proofreading:

- Check your work one sentence at a time and make sure each sentence makes complete sense.
- Check your work for any homophone errors or errors that you commonly make.
- Swap your work with a partner and ask them to annotate your work (in pencil) with suggestions or corrections.

Features of good/competent writing

- varied sentence structure and mostly accurate sentence control and a range of punctuation
- most spelling and tenses are accurate, with developing vocabulary
- clear understanding of task, purpose, format and audience
- content is developed with appropriate reasons
- writing organized into paragraphs with an overall fluency

Features of excellent/sophisticated writing

- all sentences are effective and accurate
- a range of punctuation is used effectively
- wide range of ambitious vocabulary, with accurate spelling
- sophisticated understanding of task, purpose, format and audience
- ambitious content, convincingly developed

4 CONNECTING THE DOTS

In this chapter you will focus on your ability to look back on what you have learned and to apply that knowledge. In the three previous chapters you had the opportunity to learn many skills, and by engaging with some of the activities you will have developed both as a reader and a writer. Many of the skills you have learned are transferable, not just to different areas of English, but to other areas of your life and studies. Sometimes you will need to connect and combine the skills you have learned in order to achieve your aims. The ability to evaluate, for instance, which you practised and developed in Chapter 3, is a skill that you will use in many other school subjects and in your daily life.

Here, you will revisit some of the skills you have learned in order to make connections between them. If this sounds like revision, that's because it is! The revision unit of this chapter contains activities that will use some of the things you have learned and will make connections between them.

In the exam unit you will find a breakdown of what happens for GCSE English Language assessment and two practice exam papers with some guidance on how to approach them.

Revision

Revision can be defined as 'the process of revisiting work in preparation for an exam', and the ability to revise and remember skills you have learned is just as important in the study of English as in other subjects. English revision can take a number of forms, but it will essentially be based on practising the skills you have acquired and applying them in as many different situations as you can. While memorizing key information (such as features of persuasive writing or literary techniques) can be useful and help you to feel confident,

'You can't connect the dots looking forward; you can only connect them looking backwards. So you have to trust that the dots will somehow connect in your future.' *Steve Jobs*

'The test of a first-rate intelligence is the ability to hold two opposed ideas in the mind at the same time, and still retain the ability to function.' *F. Scott Fitzgerald*

'Creativity is the power to connect the seemingly unconnected.' *William Plomer*

it is most important that you expose yourself to a wide range of reading and writing experiences. Applying your skills in response to different texts will give you the confidence to be unfazed by whatever is presented in an exam.

Read as much as you can – and not just what is suggested in English lessons. Read fiction, non-fiction, things you know you like and new genres you have never tried. Keep in mind what you are learning in the classroom and ask those same questions about what you are reading at home. Making connections and using your English skills will help to make the exams less scary. Reading widely will also allow you to experience different writing styles, and give you ideas about how to structure and punctuate your work and develop your vocabulary.

Revision

1 Recap on text and context

Learning objectives

- To distinguish between types of text
- To make connections between text and **context**
- To recap on the features of different texts

Key terms

Context: the words that come before and after a particular word or phrase and help to clarify its meaning; the circumstances or background against which something happens. For a written text this might be when it was written, who wrote it or its purpose

Skimming: reading through a text quickly to get an overall impression of what it's about, rather than trying to take in all the detail. You might skim-read a newspaper article to see if it is something you want to read more closely

Scanning: a reading technique that consists of looking quickly through a text to find specific details, rather than reading it closely to take in all the information. You might scan a train timetable for the name of your destination, rather than reading carefully through the whole thing

Introduction

It would be impossible to revise everything that is important in this book in just a couple of pages. Instead, this unit will show you how to pick out and apply some of the skills you have learned, so you can go on to do this on your own. Some connections between what you have learned will be made in order to demonstrate what can be done. It is then up to you to apply it elsewhere and to make further connections between your learning. In short, what you cover with your revision is up to you.

You have already learned some important skills for revising and recapping important information. Think back to Chapter 1, where you studied different reading techniques. The techniques of **skimming** and **scanning** are crucial when recapping details that you have learned: they will help you to locate information and key points quickly. You will be able to use these skills to access quickly what you have read and written during this course and isolate the details that you need.

Activity 1

You will take two exams in English Language. In order that you fully understand how these exams work, it is essential that you are able to identify and make judgements about the types of texts you are reading. First of all, can you identify whether it is a 'continuous' or 'non-continuous' text? Next, can you work out what type of text it is? You can often do this by thinking about why it was written and who is its intended reader.

1. Using your skills in skimming and scanning, glance through Chapters 1 and 2, and jot down what we mean by continuous and non-continuous texts.

2. List as many different examples of text types that you can think of, e.g. *description*.

Activity 2

Look at the texts below and on pages 146–147. Identify whether they are examples of continuous or non-continuous texts. Copy the table below and quickly complete the 'continuous or non-continuous?' column.

	Continuous or non-continuous?	Text type	Features of text type	Context (Think about the background to the text and anything that may have influenced the writer.)
Text 1				
Text 2				
Text 3				
Text 4				
Text 5				
Text 6				
Text 7				
Text 8				

Activity 3

Now look more closely at each of the eight texts.

a) Complete the 'Text type' column of the table, which identifies what kind of text each one is.

b) Note down in the 'Features of text type' column any details that helped you to work out what kind of text you were looking at.

Text 2

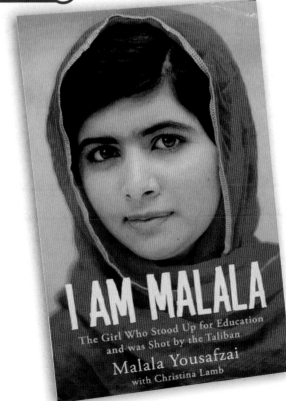

Text 1

Text 3

Anna stands up and walks slowly round the gallery, coming to a stop in front of an old man, his white beard and turban set off against a wall of golden brick hung with pages of white, inscribed paper. Before him, on the floor, robed in vivid reds and blues, sit the children he teaches. A sun-striped cat reclines on a green cushion watching a pair of doves pecking at the spangled mat. In the half-open doorway, the smallest of the children hesitates.

In the street, Anna starts to hurry. It is four o'clock and the light is fading fast.

Text 4

HOME   **ALL ABOUT ME**   **TRAVEL BLOG**   **TRAVEL TIPS**   **CONTACT**

Rediscovering America

By Sanjit | Published August 25th

Hello world! This month I will be rambling around the grand old United States of America, exploring the vast prairies, bustling cities and Grand Canyons of this star-spangled country.

First stop: New York – the city that never sleeps. No matter how many times I have visited NYC, I never tire of it. There is an indescribable buzz and energy to the city. Walking through the luminous Times Square, it almost feels like home. I can't wait to share my experiences with you!

Text 5

The Fault In Our Stars
Dying Young (Adult)

Plot
At a support group, teenaged cancer sufferer Hazel (Woodley) meets and falls for chirpy amputee Gus (Elgort). After introducing Gus to her favourite novel, Hazel is excited when he befriends the author by email. Will the pair meet their hero? The story eventually finds Gus using a Make-A-Wish-style arrangement to fly Hazel and himself to Amsterdam, where they meet the alcoholic, scornful author. Along the way, Gus and Hazel grow closer than ever, even as their disease continues to impact their lives.

Review
A teen cancer drama is like a rite of passage for a former child actress these days: Dakota Fanning did it in *Now Is Good*; now Shailene Woodley stars as a cancer patient with a similar desire to live life to the full while she can. [...]

While 16-year-old Hazel narrates, this also takes a look at the effect her condition has on her family. Laura Dern puts in a sensitive performance as the kindly, smiling mother fighting back the tears, torn between indulging her daughter and protecting her. Like the (bestselling) source novel by John Green, *The Fault In Our Stars* explores characters as much by what they don't say as what they do. Hazel's parents' strained faces speak volumes; as do Gus's cavalier jokes that help him avoid the truth.

Performances are likable and the casting's on the money: Elgort (Woodley's brother in *Divergent*) has a flirtatious sparkle while not an obvious hunk, while Woodley maintains the fresh-faced girl-next-door look that should win over the young target market. It's also quite brave for a mass-market film to feature a heroine wearing a breathing tube throughout.

Verdict
Despite a few missteps this is a spirited, touching romance and Shailene Woodley's best performance yet. *Divergent* fans after a weepie need look no further.

Text 6

Dear Editor,

I am a 17-year-old student. Despite what I read in the papers, I am fairly certain I am not a mindless idiot getting drunk in the park and trolling celebrities on Twitter.

It may surprise some of your readers, but I do try to think about other people. Two of these people are my nan and granddad who I regularly visit and enjoy spending time with. They are not rich, but they do not complain about what they have. However I think it's time someone stood up and complained for them.

Their council tax goes up, their fuel bills go up, but the service they receive goes down. Their home help rarely arrives on time, sometimes leaving my disabled nan stuck in bed for hours with my granddad fretting that he's not able to lift her himself. Now they're being told they may need to pay to go to their day centre and meet their friends. This is an appalling way to repay their years of hard work and commitment to this country.

Instead of patting themselves on the back and awarding themselves fat pay rises, why don't our politicians open their eyes and think about how other people have to live?

Yours faithfully,

Sean O'Grady

Text 7

Old Marley was as dead as a door-nail.

Mind! I don't mean to say that I know, of my own knowledge, what there is particularly dead about a door-nail. I might have been inclined, myself, to regard a coffin-nail as the deadest piece of ironmongery in the trade. But the wisdom of our ancestors is in the simile; and my unhallowed hands shall not disturb it, or the Country's done for. You will therefore permit me to repeat, emphatically, that Marley was as dead as a door-nail.

Scrooge knew he was dead? Of course he did. How could it be otherwise? Scrooge and he were partners for I don't know how many years. Scrooge was his sole executor, his sole administrator, his sole assign, his sole residuary legatee, his sole friend, and sole mourner. And even Scrooge was not so dreadfully cut up by the sad event, but that he was an excellent man of business on the very day of the funeral, and solemnised it with an undoubted bargain.

Text 8

Activity 4

In Chapter 2 you learned that looking at the context of vocabulary choice means looking at the words and phrases around a word to help you understand its meaning. Looking at the context of a piece of writing involves using a similar skill. This refers to the influences on and circumstances or background in which a text is created. Sometimes it is possible to make an informed judgement about the context of a piece of writing from clues in the text.

Have another look at texts 1–8 and note down in the 'Context' column of the table on page 145 anything you can work out about their background from the information given.

2 Reading skills

Learning objectives

- To identify the skills you have dovoloped in earlier chapters
- To think about how those skills can be used

Skills can be defined as something we have the ability to do well. How then do we gain skills? Some people seem naturally able to do certain things, whereas others have to work much harder. However talented someone is, they can always improve by developing their skills. For example, footballers must take care of their bodies, practise and train, and musicians must spend hours refining their technique.

You have learned many skills in English, but you should not assume that you can now use those skills to the best of your ability. You will only be able to fully realize your ability by practising what you have learned, applying your skills to different situations and thinking about how you can take them further.

You need to know what you have learned in order to practise it. It might seem like hard work to think back over activities and lessons you have completed over the last year, but by actively doing this you will be forced to focus on your own learning and skills.

Activity 1

You are going to make a checklist of the skills you have gained while using this book that you might need to demonstrate in an exam. Use the table below as a starting point. A few of the boxes have been filled in with examples. Try to find at least 12 different skills. Keep in mind that you may have practised these skills in more than one chapter, and in more than one way, or you may have practised them in other class-based activities. Make sure you make this clear in your table.

Chapter when practised	Skills learned	Example/explanation	Why is this important?
1	Recognizing different reading techniques	I know the difference between skimming, scanning and close reading.	I know how and when to use these skills to get to the meaning of a text.
1,2	Knowledge of how to locate information from different kinds of continuous texts		
1	Understanding of the importance of word choice		
2	How to interpret information from non-continuous texts		
3	Using the context of a sentence to work on the meaning of unfamiliar words		
3	How to evaluate my reactions to a piece of writing		

Activity 2

Read the extract below.

1. Using some of the skills you identified in Activity 1, try to write ten questions about this extract that would provide a varied test of skills for a future Year 10 student.

2. Find or write a related piece of writing which features non-continuous text to pair with this article. It could be something connected to safety and microwave ovens. Then write an additional two questions to test a future Year 10 student, based on your new text.

HOME   NEWS   ARTICLES   DOWNLOADS   SEARCH

Experience: my microwave nearly killed me

It was the week of my 32nd birthday last September. I had been at a friend's house on Saturday night for some cake and cava. I came home to my flat in Pimlico and went more or less straight to bed. I didn't wake up until the Sunday, when I found myself in intensive care.

I have no memory of it, but I'm told that just after 11pm, about half an hour after I'd gone to bed, my microwave had exploded. It was empty, plugged in and switched on at the mains, as usual. The washing machine, which was beneath it, caught fire from the explosion. The fire spread. The firefighters found me in the hallway – I must have tried to escape. I had passed out because of the carbon monoxide. [...]

They took me to intensive care, where I was in and out of a coma for three days. It was like lying in a black room, just waiting. I remember feeling shocked because I felt weightless, but also feeling very peaceful. It was like being underwater. A policeman was sent to my parents' house in Swansea to inform them what had happened. They were told that I was probably going to die, and rushed straight to London where the hospital staff told them I would live but that I would have brain damage and need 24-hour nursing care.

Thankfully, they were wrong. On the Friday I woke up for a few seconds.
I remember feeling outraged that I was naked with all these people around me. [...]

After nine days in hospital, I moved back to Swansea with my parents for two weeks. That was tough. I am very independent, so I found it hard letting them do basic things. I was so tired I couldn't climb stairs. Lifting a fork to my mouth was an effort. By the second week, I was getting my strength back slowly, and I was then well enough to move in with a friend in London.

I went back to work as a mental health nurse after a month. My family said it was too soon, but I thought I was fine. I didn't like telling people what had happened in case they thought I was being a drama queen. But on the second day my manager asked me how I was and I just burst into tears. I wasn't ready.

Six weeks after the fire, I went back to my flat for the first time. It was a shell. Everything smelled terrible. I salvaged a few books. The insurance organized the rebuilding, and it took seven months to do all the repairs. I moved back in at the end of April last year. That was an awful time. It wasn't losing all my stuff, but coming to terms with nearly dying. I felt as if I was at risk all the time, as if the sky might fall on my head. I kept my door unlocked and I got rid of all my electrical goods. I couldn't see the point of life, because I realized that I could lose it all in just one moment.

I was diagnosed with post-traumatic stress disorder and I had counselling for four months, which really helped. Gradually, I learned to change the way I approached things. I began to think that, in case I died in the next five minutes, I should make the next four minutes and 59 seconds count. I made my flat my home again and even started to be able to laugh about it. I eventually realized how impractical life was without a fridge and a washing machine, so I started using them again, but I do switch off all electrical goods at the mains every night. I will never get another microwave, though. People tell me they're unhealthy anyway.

③ Recap on writing

Learning objectives

- To identify some of the writing skills you have learned
- To think about what you can do to develop your skills

Although these two pages deal specifically with writing skills, you should keep in mind that your writing ability will naturally be influenced by what you have read. The more you read, the better your writing will become. In developing your reading skills, you are becoming more aware of what a writer does to produce an engaging, informative or entertaining piece of writing. You can then use these skills yourself. Reading and writing are linked, and what you learn in one is relevant to both.

Activity 1

You have learned about and practised many different kinds of writing during your time in school. This book has included some of them and you will have come across others in previous lessons in English or other subjects. Match the writing activities and definitions below, and write them out in the correct order.

A Story/Narrative	**1** A complete piece of writing that discusses a specific topic
B Letter	**2** Writing on a given topic that is intended to form a talk to a given audience
C Review	**3** A printed sheet of information on a given topic
D Article	**4** A written message that is sent from one person to another
E Description	**5** Writing an account of an incident – either true or invented
F Speech	**6** Writing that shows what something is like (for example, a person or a place)
G Leaflet	**7** An assessment or evaluation of the merits of something

Activity 2

Are there any other types of writing that you have encountered or that you can think of? Add these to your list and write a brief explanation of what that type of writing involves.

The definitions above are quite general and can be improved on. In order to do this it is important that we consider some key concepts or ideas. These ideas will be familiar to you, but you should still consider them carefully. Understanding each of these concepts is an important part of your achievement in English and should not be underestimated.

Key writing concepts

Audience: the person or people a piece of writing is intended for. In non-fiction writing this can be quite specific, for example, a letter could be written to a friend/relative or as a complaint to a specific company. There are many potential audiences for a piece of non-fiction writing and recognizing who your audience is will enable you to make important decisions about how to write.

Purpose: the reason for a piece of writing. Does it intend to persuade or inform the reader? Is it being written to entertain or to enable the reader to imagine something? There are many reasons for writing, and being clear on what those reasons are will enable you to respond to a task with clarity and focus.

Format: how you set out your piece of writing. In some writing you will not need to think beyond the structure of your writing and whether it is paragraphed with clarity and for effect. Other pieces will require more emphasis on headings and titles. In some areas of writing (for example, letter writing) there are specific rules. Are you certain what those are?

Formal/informal: Formal writing is writing that is addressed to an audience you don't know or whose purpose needs to be taken seriously, for example, a letter to a newspaper or a report on the facilities in your school. Informal writing can be more personal or lively, perhaps because you are more familiar with your audience or you are writing in a more relaxed way. Formality affects your choice of language, tone and literary techniques.

Exam link

The more you know about what is expected from different pieces of writing (and some of the different routes a type of writing can take) the better equipped you will be in an exam. Knowledge of the key writing concepts will enable you to work out quickly what a question is asking of you and the factors that you must keep in mind when planning your response.

Activity 3

Look back at the explanations you gave for each writing type in Activities 1 and 2. Think about how you can develop these explanations by including the key writing concepts described on page 151.

Now write a paragraph to explain each of the writing types from Activities 1 and 2, making sure you include references to the key writing concepts on page 151.

Keep in mind that for some writing types it may not be possible to specify all details, but you may have to consider others in more than one way. For example, in a fictional piece you might not be able to identify a particular audience unless you have elected to write in a specific genre (for example, science fiction), but some non-fiction pieces may be aimed at a variety of different audiences.

Support

Here is an example of how you might begin:

> An article is a complete piece of writing that discusses a specific topic. The audience that an article is aimed at can vary from something very broad like the general public (for example, a newspaper article) to something much more specific like a particular age group or fans of a specific sport or hobby (for example, a formula-one racing magazine). Similarly, it is not possible to define the purpose of an article in only one way: it may aim to inform its audience or...

In addition to the importance of understanding what is expected of you and careful planning of a piece of written work, it is essential that you pay attention to the technical accuracy of your writing. During the course of this book you have undertaken activities in proofreading, improving the accuracy of your vocabulary choices and spelling, and improving your use of sentences and key punctuation. It is very important to improve and practise your skills in this area: half your marks in Section B Writing rely on your ability to write accurately.

Activity 4

It is often quite easy to mark and correct someone else's work, but less easy to improve something you have produced yourself. Using a whole piece of writing you have produced in the last three months, do the following:

1. Circle any spelling errors and write the correct spelling in the margin.

2. Underline any errors in punctuation/grammar (for example, missing full stops, comma splicing, inaccurately punctuated speech, inaccurate tenses or agreement, inconsistent tenses).

3. Highlight any areas where you think you could improve your use of punctuation or grammar. For example, could you make your meaning sharper or offer more emphasis through the way you structure your writing?

4. Put a 'v' next to any words that you think would benefit from more specific or appropriate vocabulary.

5. Put a * next to any areas where you don't think you have made your meaning as clear or developed as you could have done.

Activity 5

Rewrite three paragraphs from your piece of work, using the corrections and suggestions you have made above. They can be consecutive paragraphs or paragraphs taken from different parts of your assignment.

The exams

4 What to expect from your exams

Learning objectives

- To familiarize yourself with the ways you will be assessed
- To understand the structure of your assessment

Introduction

Your exams will seem much less scary if you know exactly what to expect from them. The chapters in this book were written to provide instruction, advice and practice to help you to become a rounded and competent student of English language. Everything you have studied is relevant to what you need to know for a GCSE English Language exam. As you approach the end of this book, this is a good time to consider what form that assessment will take.

Summary of Assessment

Unit 1

What is tested?	*Oracy*
How is it tested?	*Through your work in class*
What is it worth?	*20% of qualification*
How is it broken down?	*Task 1 – Individual Researched Presentation (40 marks)*
	You need to complete an individual, researched presentation, which may include responses to questions and feedback, based on WJEC set themes.
	Task 2 – Responding and Interacting (40 marks)
	You need to take part in one group discussion to written and/or visual stimuli provided by WJEC to initiate the discussion.
	For both tasks, half of the marks are for the choice of register, grammatical accuracy and sentence structures used. The other half are for content and organization.

The ability to communicate fluently through speaking and listening.

Material which provokes a discussion.

How accurately and precisely you speak is just as important as what you say – half your marks will be awarded for this.

Unit 2

What is tested?	*Reading and Writing: Description, Narration and Exposition*
How is it tested?	*Written examination, 2 hours*
What is it worth?	*40% of qualification*
How is it broken down?	*Section A – Reading (40 marks)*

This section will use structured questions to test the reading of at least one description, one narration and one exposition text, including continuous and non-continuous texts.

This section will also include an editing task focusing on understanding short texts at word, sentence and text level (2.5% of qualification total – 5 of the 40 marks available).

Section B – Writing (40 marks)

This section will test description, narration or exposition writing through one writing task from a choice of two.

This section will also include one proofreading task focusing on writing accurately (2.5% of qualification total – 5 of the 40 marks available).

Half of the marks for this Writing section are for the communication and organization of writing. The other half are for writing accurately.

Reading and writing of description, narration and exposition texts.

This is worth 40% of the total qualification.

It is likely that there will be more than one of some types of texts.

Some texts will be continuous (written in sentences and paragraphs) and some will be non-continuous (information presented in a different way, e.g. lists, graphs, charts).

This will focus on understanding how the construction of words, sentences and whole texts work together to create meaning.

For the Writing section you will produce only ONE task but it will be from a choice of TWO.

This will involve identifying and correcting errors in writing.

This means that half your marks will be awarded for spelling, punctuation and grammar.

Unit 3

What is tested?	*Reading: Argumentation, Persuasion and Instructional*
	Writing: Argumentation and Persuasion
How is it tested?	*Written examination, 2 hours*
What is it worth?	*40% of qualification*
How is it broken down?	*Section A – Reading (40 marks)*

This section will use structured questions to test the reading of at least one argumentation, one persuasion and one instructional text, including continuous and non-continuous texts.

Section B – Writing (40 marks)

This section will test one compulsory argumentation writing task and one compulsory persuasion writing task.

Half of the marks for this Writing section are for the communication and organization of writing. The other half are for writing accurately.

Reading of argumentation, persuasion and instructional texts; writing of argumentation and persuasion texts.

This is worth 40% of the total qualification.

It is likely that there will be more than one of some types of texts.

Some texts will be continuous (written in sentences and paragraphs) and some will be non-continuous (information presented in a different way, e.g. lists, graphs, charts).

There will be TWO writing tasks to complete – one a persuasion writing task and the other an argumentation writing task.

This means that half your marks will be awarded for spelling, punctuation and grammar.

5 How to approach Unit 2

Learning objective

- To develop awareness of what to expect in the Unit 2 exam

You are about to see what the Unit 2 exam paper will look like. Exposure to different exam papers and practice at timing yourself will be helpful in preparing you for what is to come next year. For now, it is important that you take on board some essential information that will help you tackle your first practice paper.

Important information

On the front cover of your Unit 2 exam paper you will be told the following:

- You have 2 hours to complete the exam paper.

- This exam will also contain extra Resource Material for use in Section A.

- You should answer **all** of the questions in Section A (Reading).

- You should select only **one** title to use in Section B (Writing).

- The number of marks each question is worth will be written in brackets at the end of the question.

- You should time your approach carefully. You are advised to spend your time as follows:

Section A	– about 10 minutes reading
	– about 50 minutes answering the questions
Section B1	– about 10 minutes reading
B2	– about 10 minutes planning
	– about 40 minutes writing.

 Exam Tip How to start the Unit 2 exam successfully

Don't panic and don't rush to answer without taking some simple steps at the start. Before you begin, make sure you have thought about the following:

Section A

1. Work through the exam paper at an even pace, keeping an eye on the time. Be aware that after an hour you will need to move on to Section B.

2. Check how many marks a question is worth – you will probably need to spend more time on a question that is worth 10 marks than one that is worth 5 or 2 marks.

3. Read the question carefully – make sure you know what you are being asked to do.

4. Make sure you know which text you have been asked to look at.

5. Use a pencil or highlighter when reading the text to highlight key evidence that will help you answer the question.

6. Re-read the question – be absolutely sure that you know what you are being asked to do.

7. Track carefully through the relevant lines of the relevant text when answering the question.

8. If you are asked to compare two texts in the same question make sure you identify which one you are referring to when answering.

Section B

1. Read both options for B2. Think carefully about which one appeals to you and which one you think you could write about in some detail.

2. Choose your title.

3. Spend a few minutes planning your work and how it will develop.

4. Try to leave enough time to finish properly rather than just stopping because you've run out of time.

5. Don't write for the sake of it because you've got a few minutes spare. Keeping your reader interested is important.

6. Use any remaining time to proofread your work – writing at speed means you are likely to have made errors.

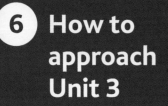

6 How to approach Unit 3

Learning objective

- To develop awareness of what to expect in the Unit 3 exam

You are also about to see what the Unit 3 exam paper will look like. As with Unit 2 it is important to take the opportunity to look at different exam papers and practice timing yourself when answering questions. Following is some essential information that will help you tackle your first practice paper.

Important information

On the front cover of your Unit 3 exam paper you will be told the following:

- You have 2 hours to complete the exam.
- This exam will also contain extra Resource Material for use in Section A.
- You should answer **all** of the questions in Section A (Reading).
- You should answer **both** of the questions in Section B (Writing).
- The number of marks each question is worth will be written in brackets at the end of the question.
- You should time your approach carefully. You are advised to spend your time as follows:

  Section A – about 10 minutes reading
  – about 50 minutes answering the questions

  Section B – about 10 minutes planning (approximately 5 minutes per question)
  – about 50 minutes writing (approximately 25 minutes per question).

Exam Tip **How to start the Unit 3 exam successfully**

Don't panic and don't rush to answer without taking some simple steps at the start. Before you begin, make sure you have thought about the following:

Section A

1. Work through the exam paper at an even pace, keeping an eye on the time. Be aware that after an hour you will need to move on to Section B.
2. Check how many marks a question is worth – you will probably need to spend more time on a question that is worth 10 marks than one that is worth 5 or 2 marks.
3. Read the question carefully – make sure you know what you are being asked to do.
4. Make sure you know which text you have been asked to look at.
5. Use a pencil or highlighter when reading the text to highlight key evidence that will help you answer the question.

6. Re-read the question – be absolutely sure that you know what you are being asked to do.
7. Track carefully through the relevant lines of the relevant text when answering the question.
8. If you are asked to compare two texts in the same question make sure you identify which one you are referring to when answering.

Section B

1. Read the relevant questions carefully.
2. Make sure you are clear on the purpose and audience of your piece of writing.
3. Spend a few minutes planning your work – have an idea of the points you want to make and in what order.
4. Try to leave enough time to finish properly rather than just stopping because you've run out of time.
5. Remember you have two writing questions to complete.
6. Use any remaining time to proofread your work – writing at speed means you are likely to have made errors.

Assessment

Sample Unit 2 exam paper

SECTION A (Reading): 40 marks

*In the **separate Resource Material** (pages 161–165) there are five texts on the theme of 'Running' labelled **Text A–E**. Read each text carefully and answer **all** the questions below that relate to each of the texts.*

TEXT A

A1.   By what percentage had the popularity of men's marathon running increased in the time period?   [1]

A2.   In which continent had marathon running most increased in popularity?   [1]

A3.   The information refers to 'Top & Bottom Performing Countries'. Select one definition from the list below that best defines the word 'performing' in this context.   [1]

    a) increasing in size

    b) a way of entertaining people

    c) doing something to a particular standard

    d) doing something efficiently

TEXT B

A4.   How regularly does 'parkrun' take place?   [1]

A5.   What is meant in the second paragraph when Ben Smith describes the runners' feet as 'tapping the grass'?   [1]

A6.   What does Ben Smith say about the runners who take part in 'parkrun'?   [5]

TEXT C

A7. Who is the NHS 'Couch to 5k' plan aimed at? [1]

    a) serious runners

    b) people suffering from type 2 diabetes

    c) the over-50s

    d) everyone

A8. Identify two ways someone can benefit from following the 'Couch to 5k' plan. How does the article suggest these benefits will improve their lives? [4]

TEXT D

A9. Identify three ways that Ronnie O'Sullivan thinks running is different from snooker. [3]

A10. Which other sportsman does Ronnie say was also obsessed with running 10 kilometres? [1]

A11. How did Ronnie feel about joining the running club? [5]

You must use evidence from the text to support your answer.

TEXT E

A12. In the opening line the narrator refers to the time of the morning as being 'when even birds haven't the heart to whistle'. [1]

Select one explanation from the list below which best describes what he means.

    a) the birds are too cold to whistle

    b) it is still night time and there are no sounds

    c) he's dreamy and still half asleep

    d) it's so early the birds haven't started to sing

A13. How do Ronnie O'Sullivan and the narrator of 'The Loneliness of the Long Distance Runner' present the sport of running in Text D and Text E? [10]

You must refer to both texts to support your comments on the language the writers have used.

Editing (5 marks)

In this part of the paper you will be assessed for the quality of your understanding and editing skills.

1. Read the paragraph below and then answer the questions that follow:

    It was .....(1)..... to know what to do first. Sophie surveyed the scene and tried to prioritize where her cleaning would .....(2)..... .

    (a) Circle the word below that best fits gap (1):

         A) intrinsic   B) difficult   C) easy   D) obvious   [1]

    (b) Circle the word below that best fits gap (2):

         A) begin   B) end   C) gleam   D) finalize   [1]

2. Circle the pair of words that best fit the meaning of the sentence below: [1]

    Jamie was .... as he climbed out of the car; his race was .... and now there was just the long walk back to the garage to look forward to.

    (A) delighted...beginning

    (B) distraught...over

    (C) pleased...finished

    (D) upset...next

    (E) mortified...fast

3. Read the text below which consists of sentences in the wrong order and show your understanding by answering the questions that follow:
    1. He knew that this was the source of so many of his most delicious creations.
    2. Mark entered the spotless kitchen, clutching his favourite recipe book.
    3. Frantically, he whipped through the pages in a quest for something bigger and better.
    4. His eyes lit up at the sight of a chocolate show stopper – this was it!
    5. But this time it had to be even more special.

    (a) Which sentence should come second in the text? Write the number of the sentence below.   [1]

    (b) Which sentence should come fourth in the text? Write the number of the sentence below.   [1]

Resource Material for use with Section A

TEXT A shows the results on research into the growing popularity of marathon running worldwide.

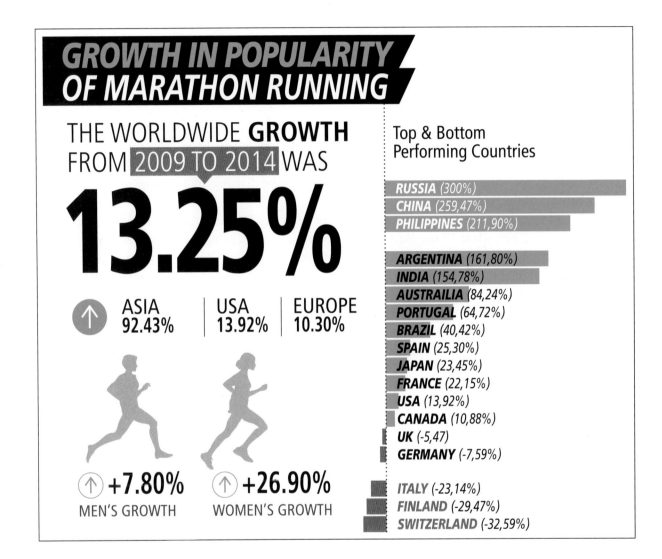

GROWTH IN POPULARITY OF MARATHON RUNNING

THE WORLDWIDE **GROWTH** FROM 2009 TO 2014 WAS

13.25%

↑ ASIA 92.43% | USA 13.92% | EUROPE 10.30%

↑ +7.80% MEN'S GROWTH

↑ +26.90% WOMEN'S GROWTH

Top & Bottom Performing Countries

RUSSIA (300%)
CHINA (259,47%)
PHILIPPINES (211,90%)

ARGENTINA (161,80%)
INDIA (154,78%)
AUSTRAILIA (84,24%)
PORTUGAL (64,72%)
BRAZIL (40,42%)
SPAIN (25,30%)
JAPAN (23,45%)
FRANCE (22,15%)
USA (13,92%)
CANADA (10,88%)
UK (-5,47)
GERMANY (-7,59%)

ITALY (-23,14%)
FINLAND (-29,47%)
SWITZERLAND (-32,59%)

TEXT B is an extract from an article by runner Ben Smith for The Guardian *newspaper.*

A parkrun is an unusual, even beautiful sight

Stand on the corner of Park Road and Chestnut Avenue at 9am on a Saturday, look south, and a kilometre away through the misty morning stillness a dark, rumbling cloud is visible, closing fast. Out of the centre of it, on the wide strip of grass between the road and the trees, colours emerge, then shapes, and just as you [...] consider diving for cover, you hear the thunder of feet: runners.

At first it's the quick ones, small and light, their feet tapping the grass as they pass. Then the rest come, almost 1,000 of them pouring past, the individual shapes now more varied, young and old, fat and thin, breathing hard already as they turn a right angle on to the path with 4k to go. Then they are gone, stretching out into the distance like bunting around the perimeter of the park.

It's an unusual, even beautiful sight, seen here in Bushy Park, south-west London, every week since 2004, when 13 people turned up. Now parkrun is a huge weekly event, with dozens of sister runs across the world. Most of them are not like Bushy. [...] Most are more like that original event, a flashmob of a few dozen ordinary joggers who happen to be doing their three weekend miles in the same park at the same time.

But even the smaller ones share a spirit and a remarkably broad cast. [...] You can usually rely on seeing pensioners, kids, groups of mates, parkrun addicts (who wear T-shirts testifying to their 50th, 100th or 250th event) and usually, on the flatter courses, at least one parent pushing a buggy. [...]

There are also serious athletes – the Bushy Park course record is held by Olympic 1500m runner Andy Baddeley (Mo Farah is 20th) – and even small events can offer a humbling chance to see that, however well your training is going, there is someone who lives down the road from you who can run 5k in the 15 minutes or so it takes to walk to the corner shop and back.

TEXT C is taken from information published by the NHS to encourage people to start running.

NHS

Get running with Couch to 5K

Taking up running can seem like a scary prospect, especially if you feel out of shape or unfit.

But did you know that regular running can help reduce the risk of chronic illnesses such as heart disease, type 2 diabetes and stroke, boost your mood and keep your weight under control?

The NHS Couch to 5K plan is designed to get you off the couch and gradually work you up to running 5K or for half an hour, in just nine weeks.

What is Couch to 5K?

Couch to 5K is a running plan developed to help absolute beginners get into running. The beginners' running plan was developed by a novice runner, Josh Clark, who wanted to help his fifty-something mum get off the couch and start running too. The plan involves three runs per week, with a day of rest in between, with a different schedule for each of the nine weeks.

How does Couch to 5K work?

Probably the biggest challenge a novice runner faces is not knowing how or where to start. Often when trying to get into exercise, we can overdo it, feel defeated and give up when we're just getting started. Couch to 5K works because it starts with a mix of running and walking, to gradually build up your fitness and stamina. Week one involves running for just a minute at a time, creating realistic expectations and making the challenge feel achievable right from the start.

Who is Couch to 5K for?

Couch to 5K is for everyone. Whether you've never run before, or if you want to get back into being more active, Couch to 5K is a free and easy way of getting fitter and healthier. If you have any health concerns about beginning an exercise regime such as Couch to 5K, make an appointment to see your GP and discuss it with them first.

What are the benefits?

There are plenty of benefits from getting into running. For starters, it's an easy way of improving your physical health. Running regularly will improve the health of your heart and lungs. It can also help you lose weight, especially if combined with a healthy diet.

There is evidence it may help increase bone density in some people, which can help protect against bone diseases such as osteoporosis.

There are also mental benefits of running. Taking on the challenge of Couch to 5K can help boost your confidence and self-belief, as you prove that you can set yourself a target and achieve a goal. Running regularly can also be a great stress reliever and has even been shown to combat depression.

TEXT D is an extract from World Snooker Champion Ronnie O'Sullivan's autobiography called Running. *Here he describes his first experiences of running with a club.*

The first time I went down to the club I was a bit shy. I didn't say much, did my bit and sneaked off. But the runners were really friendly, and after two or three times they'd introduce themselves, and I'd go to the bar and have a glass of orange with them after we'd killed ourselves on the track. A few of them recognized me, but they didn't seem that interested in who I was. We never spoke about snooker; it was all running. Everyone left their job at the door. It was just about racing; who's running well. If you were into running, Tuesday night at the track was just the best thing.
[...]
   I'd been at the club around six months and was loving it. Then I started on the 10 kilometres. I don't know why 10 kilometres is such a perfect distance, but it is. I suppose it's a sprint, but still a long way. I'm not the first sportsman to get obsessed by the 10 kilometres – though maybe the others didn't to the same extent. The great England batsman Kevin Pietersen had the same thing. There was a time he was touring India, and all he seemed bothered about was getting his 10 kilometres down. He'd finish a day at a Test match, the team would get in the coach and then he'd be, like, right I'm running six miles back to the hotel.
[...]
   Running is such a different world from snooker. It's outdoors, it's physical and the very opposite of that claustrophobic snooker hall. [...] But in some ways running and snooker aren't so different. You're still on your own – you get the disappointments, you get the glory, it's all for yourself. It's still a one-man sport. Whereas snooker is all about technique, running is much more blood, guts, determination and finding something within yourself to keep going. There are times when you think you can't keep going, but you do. And after a race you swear you're never going to put yourself through that again, as you cross the finishing line, but invariably you do. It's so painful, and you just wonder what made you do it. Nearly all runners feel the same – even those who make it look easy and win all the races. But when you see you had a good race, and you're getting somewhere, and getting rewards for it, it makes it all worthwhile.

TEXT E is an extract taken from Alan Sillitoe's novel The Loneliness of the Long Distance Runner. **Here the main character describes his feelings as he sets out on an early morning run.**

As soon as I take that first flying leap out into the frosty grass of an early morning when even birds haven't the heart to whistle, I get to thinking, and that's what I like. I go my rounds in a dream, turning at lane or footpath corners without knowing I'm turning, leaping brooks without knowing they're there, and shouting good morning to the early cow-milker without seeing him. It's a treat being a long-distance runner, out in the world by yourself with not a soul to make you bad-tempered or tell you what to do [...]. Sometimes I think that I've never been so free as during the couple of hours when I'm trotting up the path out of the gates and turning by that bare-faced, big-bellied oak tree at the lane end. Everything's dead, but good, because it's dead before coming alive, not dead after being alive. That's how I look at it. Mind you, I often feel frozen stiff at first. I can't feel my hands or feet or flesh at all, like I'm a ghost who wouldn't know the earth was under him if he didn't see it now and again through the mist. But even though some people would call this frost-pain suffering [...], I don't because I know that in half an hour I'm going to be warm, that by the time I get to the main road and am turning on to the wheat-field footpath by the bus stop I'm going to feel as hot as a potbellied stove and as happy as a dog with a tin tail.

SECTION B (Writing): 40 marks

B1. *In this task you will be assessed for the quality of your proofreading.*

Read the email below that has been sent to you to confirm your booking at a campsite.

Identify the five errors and correct them on the email below.

Dear Holidaymaker,

Thank you for your booking.

Your booking reference is: CP17/AUG17/003. Please quote this on all future correspondance.

You're booking details are shown below:
Arrival Date: 05/08/2017
Departure Date: 09/08/2017
Type: Tent
Adult's: 2
Under 14s: 2
Cost: £154

The total charge for your stay is £154.00. This will be payable on arrival

If you have any questions or need to made changes to your booking please email us at lakeview@xtremecamping.co.uk or call 01225 833 522.

A copy of our campsite rules are available on our website.

We look foward to seeing you this summer.

Best wishes,

Lakeview Campsite

B2. *In this section you will be assessed for the quality of your **writing** skills.*

20 marks are awarded for communication and organization;
15 marks are awarded for writing accurately.

You should aim to write about 350–500 words.

Choose one of the following for your writing: [35]

Either,   *(a)*   Write a description of the scene at the start of a charity long-distance running race.

Or,   *(b)*   You and your friends have decided to set up a school running club. Write a speech that you intend to give in your school assembly to explain why you think other students should join you.

Sample Unit 3 exam paper

SECTION A (Reading): 40 marks

*In the separate **Resource Material** (pages 165–169) there are five texts on the theme of 'Teeth' labelled **Text A–E**. Read each text carefully and answer **all** the questions below that relate to each of the texts.*

TEXT A

A1.   By what percentage does fluoride reduce dental decay?   [1]

A2.   Which of the following foods are more likely to make us smile?   [1]

    a) Chocolate ☐

    b) Sunday roast ☐

    c) Curry ☐

    d) Fry up ☐

A3.   What is the purpose of text A?   [1]

    a) Personal use ☐

    b) Public use ☐

    c) Occupational use ☐

    d) Educational use ☐

Text B

A4.   Look at the instructions on how to look after your teeth. Put the instructions in the order that they would be best completed.   [3]

The first one has been done for you:

- Select your toothbrush and toothpaste carefully.

-

-

-

A5.   What is meant by the phrase 'superfluous toothpaste'?   [1]

    a) Excess toothpaste ☐

    b) Diluted toothpaste ☐

    c) Stale toothpaste ☐

    d) Flavoured toothpaste ☐

Text C

A6.   The writer tells us he was 'embarrassed to smile'. Explain the reasons why the writer had problems with their teeth.   [5]

A7.   The writer tells us that they managed to 'dislodge my braces'. Choose one of the following phrases that describes what this means.   [1]

    a) Their braces fell off ☐

    b) Their braces were permanently removed by the dentist ☐

    c) Their braces were displaced ☐

    d) Their braces were semi-permanent ☐ .

A8.   The writer tells us that eating chewy sweets 'exacerbated' their dental problems. Explain what is meant by the term 'exacerbated'.   [1]

Text D

A9.   Summarize what people have done to fix their dental problems.   [5]

A10.   What should you do if you are having dental problems?   [1]

Text E

A11.   How does the writer try to persuade us that parents are to blame for their children's dental problems?   [10]

Texts C–E

A12.   Using texts C–E, compare the issues that people may have with their teeth and gums.   [10]

Resource Material for use with Section A

TEXT A is a poster giving facts about oral health from the British Dental Health Foundation.

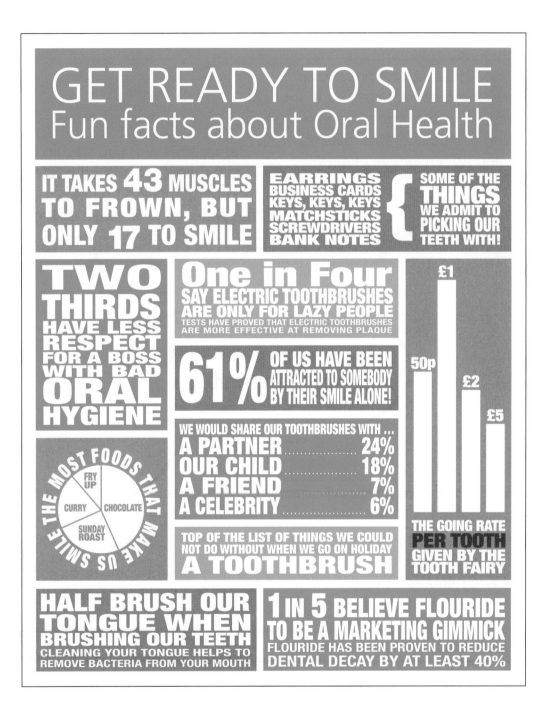

TEXT B is a series of instructions for brushing your teeth.

After brushing your teeth spit out any superfluous toothpaste. Don't rinse your mouth with water or mouthwash as it will wash away the concentrated fluoride in the remaining toothpaste, thus diluting it and reducing its preventive effects.

Before brushing you should put a pea-sized amount of toothpaste on your brush. There is no need to add any water to your brush or the paste.

Caring for your teeth in four easy steps

Make sure you brush all the surfaces of all your teeth, which should take about two minutes. Remember to brush the inside surfaces, outside surfaces and the chewing surfaces of your teeth.

Select your toothbrush and toothpaste carefully. Either an electric or manual brush is fine but opt for a small head with medium or soft bristles. Use any brand of toothpaste as long as it contains 1,350–1,500ppm (parts per million) fluoride.

TEXT C is a magazine article written by someone who has suffered with tooth decay all their life.

So embarrassed to smile...

Teeth troubles have haunted me for as long as I can remember. When I was a young child my father made no secret of the fact that he lost his teeth at the age of 30 and that his father had lost them at an even younger age. Growing up I dreaded losing my own teeth and used to attack my teeth, tongue and gums with a harsh brush every evening, which caused bleeding and inflammation of the gums.

During my teenage years I can honestly say that I did not do myself any favours. Spending my lunch money on cigarettes, sweets and fizzy drinks did not help my teeth and only caused me to get a few additional fillings. When I was 13 I had fixed metal braces fitted on my teeth and struggled to keep my teeth clean. On several occasions I managed to dislodge my braces when eating chewy sweets and this exacerbated the problem. When the braces were removed I had to have several fillings to fix the damage.

It was my University years, however, that caused most of the damage. With a limited amount of income, I did not visit the dentist for three years. When I finally got a job (I'm convinced it took longer than it should have done because I was so uncomfortable to show my teeth) I visited the dentist and was horrified by her comments. I was told that the enamel on my teeth was too thin and that I had seven cavities that required attention. The hygienist was absolutely brilliant and gave me a wealth of advice on what to eat, when to eat it and how to take care of my teeth.

Ten years on, I still have my teeth. I visit the dentist regularly and ensure that I take good care of my teeth and gums.

Children showing signs of decay

	Primary teeth		Secondary teeth	
Survey	**Age 5**	**Age 8**	**Age 12**	**Age 15**
1983	66%	80%	83%	94%
1993	51%	72%	53%	72%
2003	52%	71%	54%	65%
2013	41%	55%	52%	63%

Source: ONS/Children's Dental Health in Wales, 2013

TEXT D is a newspaper article written about do-it-yourself dentistry.

Disastrous DIY Dentistry

According to a recent survey, millions of people in England have attempted to solve their own dental problems and the results will shock many of our readers.

Cast your mind back to when you were a child. Can you remember older relatives instructing you to pull out wobbly teeth using a door handle and some string? Did you laugh at their stupidity? Well it would appear that almost 8% of British have attempted to solve their dental problems with some pretty high risk strategies.

Of those who admitted performing their own dentistry, one in four had shockingly tried to pull out a tooth using pliers. A huge number of those polled had attempted to whiten their teeth using a range of household cleaning products from scouring pads Domestos with some very painful side effects.

With changes to dental legislation in recent years, many people have struggled to find an NHS dental surgery. This has left people with no other option than to either suffer or to attempt to solve their own problems. The poll also found 12% of those who had tried DIY techniques had tried to extract a tooth by using a piece of string tied to a door handle. Some 30% of DIY dentists had tried to remove plaque with a range of household tool including penknives and needles. Other DIY procedures people admitted to included: using glue to stick down a filling or crown; popping an ulcer with a pin and trying to stick down a loose filling with chewing gum. Those suffering with detail pain were reported to have rubbed gums with alcohol or aspirin tablets. Perhaps the most inventive DIY dentist admitted to making false teeth using modelling clay.

Sadly, these DIY dentists are desperate to improve their teeth or to alleviate pain and ought to be able to find a good local dentist to solve their problems in a safe and hygienic manner. Susie Sanderson, of the British Dental Association, says: "While worries about accessing or paying for dental care can clearly be a concern, it really isn't advisable to resort to do-it-yourself care…If you are having trouble finding a dentist then contact your local health centre."

TEXT E is a web article about the cause of tooth decay in children, written by Victoria Lambert.

Rotten teeth are all the fault of Mum and Dad

Remind me, what century are we in? The news that 500 British children are admitted to hospital every week on account of rotten teeth made me think we'd slipped back to Tudor times, when you rubbed your teeth with your finger and hoped for the best.

But no, here we are in the 21st century, in which children have access to free, twice-yearly dental check-ups and school visits from grown-ups dressed as comedy molars. Our children have been exposed to YouTube tutorials on dental hygiene featuring Elsa from Frozen, and SpongeBob Square Pants toothpaste. And yet still their choppers are rotting like old vegetables in the fridge.

The figures from the Health and Social Care Information Centre (HSCIC) are alarming: 25,812 children aged five to nine were admitted to hospital for dental problems in 2013/14 – 14 per cent up on 2010/11.

Dr Carter, chief executive of the British Dental Health Foundation charity, says: 'The figures are a real representation of what is going on across the country – especially in the North West and parts of Yorkshire. Dental decay is a disease of poverty and disadvantage, very much on North–South lines.'

But he doesn't accept it is a new problem: 'If you look back 20 or 30 years, the number of children having extractions would have been far higher – the difference is that this would have been carried out in dental surgeries rather than in hospital.'

So why are our bambinos turning into real-life gummy bears? Is it the fault of the NHS? Politicians? The food industry? Worse, says Dr Carter. 'It's pure parental neglect.'

Firstly, there is diet. 'Everyone grazes constantly – we've gone from three meals a day to between seven and 10, plus sugary snacks, and all washed down with high-sugar drinks. There is a connection with the obesity crisis, but from the dental perspective, sugar is the prime culprit in dental decay.'

Decay happens when sugars in food and drinks react with the bacteria in plaque, forming acids. Every time you eat or drink anything containing sugars, acids start to soften and dissolve the enamel. Attacks can last for an hour after eating or drinking, before natural salts in saliva cause the enamel to 'remineralize' and harden again.

It's not just brightly coloured, sugary drinks that are to blame but fruit juices, too. 'An awful lot have added sugars,' he warns. 'Parents must learn to check by reading labels: anything ending in "-ose", such as sucrose, maltose or fructose is a sugar. And try to ensure children are drinking all the drink in one go – not sipping, as that constantly bathes teeth in sweetness.'

Be careful what you pack in their lunch boxes, too. 'Things parents think of as healthy can be risky, such as sultanas or dried fruit, which are not only high in sugar but also sticky, so sugar stays in the mouth longer.'

Dr Carter is also concerned that children are not taught a proper care regime at home. 'Some parents don't even provide a toothbrush or fluoride toothpaste, and don't supervise their children's cleaning regime.' Lastly, parents are not taking their children to the dentist every six months for a check-up, where early signs of decay picked up. 'If a child's first experience at the dentist is pain, and being shipped to hospital for multiple extractions, you are probably setting that child up to be dental-phobic for life.'

SECTION B (Writing): 40 marks

In this section you will be assessed for the quality of your writing skills.

*Answer **both** B1 and B2*

B1. *Use information taken from Texts A–E in the resource material and your own knowledge about tooth care. Write a lively article for a teenage audience persuading them to care for their teeth.*

10 marks are awarded for communication and organization;
10 marks are awarded for writing accurately.

You should aim to write about 200–300 words.

Write your article. [20]

B2. Text E argues that parents are to blame for rotten teeth. The following statement was written in response to this text:

'Parents are not just responsible for their children's teeth but they should be responsible for every aspect of their child's life until the age of 16. If their children break the law or misbehave, then the parents should be punished.'

You feel strongly about the statement above and decide to write a letter to your local newspaper giving your views.

Write your letter. [20]

10 marks are awarded for communication and organization;
10 marks are awarded for writing accurately.

You should aim to write about 200–300 words.

Achievement: something good or worthwhile that you have succeeded in doing

Adjectives: words like big, exciting and unexpected. They describe what is named by nouns, noun phrases or pronouns

Argumentation writing: argumentation is a form of writing which presents a view of a topic. Students will need to present a range of viewpoints on a given topic. Argumentation texts can include a letter to an editor, a report or an article about a given topic.

Chronologically: in the order in which things occurred

Compare: to note the similarity or difference between two or more things

Comparison: a consideration of the similarities or differences between two or more things

Context: the words that come before and after a particular word or phrase and help to clarify its meaning; the circumstances or background against which something happens. For a written text this might be when it was written, who wrote it or its purpose

Continuous text: text written in sentences and paragraphs

Editing: to choose material and arrange it to form a coherent whole

Evaluate: to form an idea of the state or value of something

Exaggerate: to make something seem larger, better or worse, or more important than it really is

Fact: something that is known to have happened and/or to be true

Figurative language: a word or phrase that shouldn't be taken literally, for example, 'the drying clothes waved like proud flags'. Figurative language calls on the reader to use their imagination to complete the writer's meaning and almost always takes the form of either metaphors or similes.

First person (I/we): using first-person narrative allows you to tell a story from the perspective of a character in the text. In non-fiction texts it can be seen as a biased view because it only tells one side of the story

Formal: strictly following accepted social rules; traditional, proper. A piece of formal writing is addressed to someone you are either unfamiliar with or to a formal audience, for example, a school teacher or governor

Imperative: an imperative verb is used in a sentence where a writer or speaker is giving an order or telling someone to do something. For example: Go home! You take the dog for a walk. Use your time wisely.

Impression: effect produced on the mind, ideas

Informal: not formal; unofficial or casual; everyday. A piece of informal writing is addressed to someone you are familiar or friends with

Narrative: a spoken or written account of connected events; a story

Non-continuous text: text which presents information in other ways, for example charts, tables, diagrams and graphs

Nouns: words like girl, book, Mary, school, year, money, happiness, Brighton. One of their main jobs is to identify a person, place or thing

Overview: a general summary, explanation or outline of a situation

Personification: the attribution of a personal nature or human characteristics to something nonhuman

Perspective: a particular way of thinking about something

Persuasion writing: persuasion is a form of writing which aims to convince a reader of the writer's viewpoint. It may be emotive and will seek to influence a reader's judgement. Persuasive texts can include a speech to a given audience, a letter of protest or a review of a book or film.

Persuasive writing: a form of writing which tries to convince a reader to agree with the writer's viewpoint

Purpose: the purpose of a text is what the writer deliberately sets out to achieve. They may wish to persuade, encourage, advise or even anger their reader, or a mixture of these

Reflect: to think deeply or carefully about something

Retrieve: to find or extract; to locate and bring back

Scanning: a reading technique that consists of looking quickly through a text to find specific details, rather than reading it closely to take in all the information. You might scan a train timetable for the name of your destination, rather than reading carefully through the whole thing

Simile: a figure of speech in which one thing is compared to another using the words like or as, as in He's as fit as a fiddle

Skimming: reading through a text quickly to get an overall impression of what it's about, rather than trying to take in all the detail. You might skimread a newspaper article to see if it is something you want to read more closely

Speculate: to form an opinion about something without knowing the facts

Summary: a brief document or statement that gives the main points of something. It is a shortened version of a longer text which is written up in the reader's own words. Producing a summary tests your understanding of what you have read

Synthesize: to form something by bringing together information from different sources

Third person (he/she/it/they): using third-person narrative means the story is told from an independent point of view so you can see what all of the characters think and feel. In non-fiction texts it is regarded as an unbiased voice

Topic sentence: often the first sentence in a paragraph, it tells the reader what the paragraph is about, and is followed by other sentences which give more detail

Verbal reasoning skills: skills which help you understand and comprehend information, like reason and deduction